MILITARY CARTRIDGE HEADSTAMPS

COLLECTOR'S GUIDE

— CODE BOOK —

Compiled by Charles Conklin

HERITAGE BOOKS
2007

HERITAGE BOOKS
AN IMPRINT OF HERITAGE BOOKS, INC.

Books, CDs, and more—Worldwide

For our listing of thousands of titles see our website
at
www.HeritageBooks.com

Published 2007 by
HERITAGE BOOKS, INC.
Publishing Division
65 East Main Street
Westminster, Maryland 21157-5026

Copyright © 2006 Charles Conklin

Other books by the author:
58's Are the Greatest

All rights reserved. No part of this book may be reproduced or transmitted in any form or by any means, electronic or mechanical, including photocopying, recording or by any information storage and retrieval system without written permission from the author, except for the inclusion of brief quotations in a review.

International Standard Book Number: 978-0-7884-4117-2

DEDICATION

This work is dedicated to my family,
Theresa, Barbara and Scott

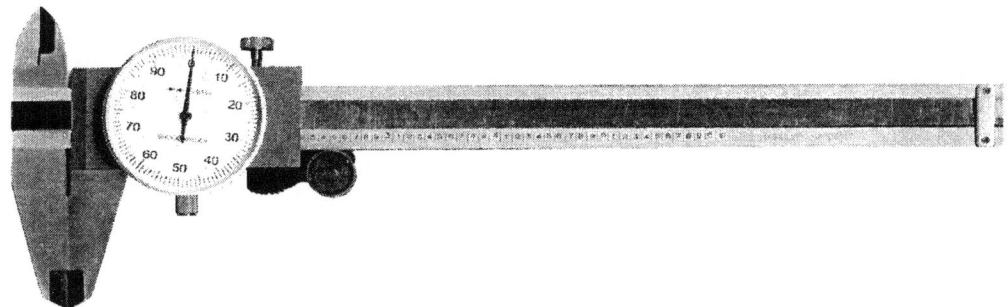

ACKNOWLEDGEMENTS

To my family in the cartridge world

William G. Gessner Sr.
Christine L. Gessner
Mora Rea

and the many kind folks at the Pennsylvania cartridge shows:

Vic Engel (Williamsport)
Paul Callow (Denver)

Charles Conklin is the co-author of "58's Are The Greatest"
The new comprehensive cartridge book (1800-1875)
By Author, William G. Gessner, Sr.

CONTENTS

Introduction …	Pages 1 - 4
Headstamp guide (by Country) …	Pages 5 - 21 & 24
U.S. Small arms inspectors …	Pages 22 - 23
Color-codes …	Pages 25 - 27
World cartridge dimension comparison table …	Pages 30 - 31
Foreign language (Key word) translation section …	Pages 32 - 35
G. Roth headstamp codes …	Pages 36 - 39
DWM headstamp codes …	Pages 40 - 45
U.S. cartridge examples …	Pages 46 - 91
Turkish cartridge example …	Page 92
Swiss cartridge example …	Page 93
Russian cartridge example …	Page 94
Japanese cartridge examples …	Pages 95 - 97
Italian cartridge examples …	Pages 98 - 101
Israeli cartridge example …	Page 102
German cartridge examples …	Pages 103 - 113
French cartridge examples …	Pages 114 - 120
Finish cartridge examples …	Pages 121 - 122
India (British rule) cartridge example …	Page 123
United Kingdom cartridge examples …	Pages 124 - 128
Netherlands cartridge example …	Page 129
Czech cartridge example (German occupation) …	Page 130
Canadian cartridge example …	Page 131
Belgium cartridge example …	Page 132
Headstamp alphabetical index …	Pages 133 – 146
Patronefabriken code index (German P-code) …	Pages 147 - 148
Bibliography …	Page 149

INTRODUCTION

These notes are the culmination of ten plus years of collecting cartridges and gathering information for my own personal use. This is not such a long time if you consider many of my fellow collectors have been doing so for 40-50-60 years and more. However, as many of them may tell you, I have always been curious as to the national origin of each cartridge and the various functions many of them were created to perform. This is probably the reason I personally enjoy collecting, that and the fact there are still unknown areas yet to be explored. I say explored because finding these origins are often difficult, since the meaning of headstamp codes are often hidden behind such obstacles as foreign languages, military secrecy, lost and destroyed records or any combination thereof.

It's easy to find several well-intentioned collectors who will volunteer information about headstamps, but when you compare your notes, you may end up more confused then when you started. This was very frustrating to me and I soon realized I was not alone. Although many collectors shrug it off by saying, "that's what makes collecting so challenging", I felt the need to group together all the information I had found and pool it into some sort of handy format I could access on the run. A great deal of the information contained in this guide, can be found in various military publications & manufacturer catalogs, but who wants to carry around ten different books at a cartridge show not to mention that cluttered desk at home.

Unfortunately, I can not guarantee that every single headstamp entry contained in this guide is completely accurate because some of them have come to me based on word of mouth or partial documentation.

My own personal interest has always been with military cartridges, especially World War I and World War II, which is why this guide so heavily favors those periods.

In addition, I hope you will find the limited section on interpreting foreign languages and their industry abbreviations useful on certain key words pertinent to decipher ammo crates as well as color / letter code systems.

Should you be new to collecting cartridges, my only advice is that you select an area of strong interest to you and see where it leads. I have seen many variations of cartridge collecting over the years and there does not seem to be a wrong way to do it unless you go off in too many directions at once and become discouraged. Make no mistake about it there is a multitude of directions to choose from; the material covered in this book span the time frame of more than two great wars and yet it remains a drop in the bucket compared to the long history of cartridges.

The information in this guide is conveyed to you in table format, which allows you to draw your own conclusions. The primary intent of this book is to serve as a convenient source of reference material for the collector while the secondary goal is to inspire new collectors who will add both information and enthusiasm to our endeavor.

You will notice the use of headstamp drawings as opposed to actual pictures; this is due to the excess space requirement needed to display a picture of sufficient resolution to be useful. However each headstamp drawing in this guide was modeled after an _actual cartridge_ I have examined and verified. The next few pages will help orient you with some of the basic ritual and terminology of cartridge identification.

The term "cartridge identification" will no doubt lead you to an exacting array of steps whose process will allow you to determine a cartridges designation in terms of it's caliber, case length, function type, date and place of manufacture or point of origin.

Cartridges generally fall into a category designation titled "small arms" consisting of specimens under 15mm. Cartridge sizes exceeding 20mm or greater constitute a scope of heavy artillery with fuzed explosive or solid monobloc projectiles not covered in this guide.

Three basic questions that summarize the information needed to attain cartridge identification and fulfill the purpose of this guide are as follows.

(1) What is the cartridge designation? This is expressed by a brief nomenclature, which includes a caliber (bullet diameter) measurement in inches or millimeters. The cartridges case length, rim diameter, case mouth diameter, bullet and case material composition as well as primer type.

(2) Who made the cartridge, and when? Some degree of accuracy can be derived from the markings that appear on most cartridge bases, which are termed "headstamps". The headstamp usually includes a year stamp or year code of manufacture, however you must keep in mind that due to both wartime shortages as well as economic reasons (changing the headstamp bunter was costly), some cartridge types (dummy cartridges / gallery rounds) were prone to being reused. The percentage of this reuse was generally small overall, so in most instances you should get an accurate assessment. If the cartridge is unmarked or the headstamp markings are inadequate or obscured, it may be possible to determine its maker by first hand comparison to known specimens by an expert.

(3) What is the cartridges specialty or function type? The possible categories are: ball, tracer, incendiary, armor piercing, explosive, gallery, dummy, blank and various combinations. Function identification may involve color codes, stamped marking, bullet shapes and other tactile features. These were often unique to the country the cartridge was manufactured in or for and also may vary from different time periods.

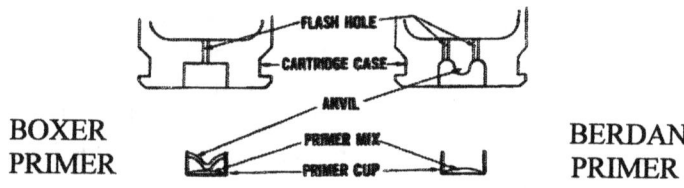

BOXER PRIMER   **BERDAN PRIMER**

1 Rimmed cartridges have an extractor flange that extends beyond the cartridge body. Some may also have a groove in the case body ahead of the rim.
2 Semirimmed cases have an extractor flange that only slightly extends beyond the cartridge body but not to the extent of the rimmed specimens. These also may an extractor groove in the case body adjacent to the rim.
3 Rimless cartridges have a rim diameter the same as the case body and does not protrude beyond it.

DEFINITION OF A CARTRIDGE

The cartridge is composed of 4 basic parts, projectile, container (case) primer and powder.

1. Projectile-made of wood, steel, lead, combination, paper blank, BB shot paper or wood, A.P., Tracer, combination, incendiary or explosive.

2. Case: brass, copper, paper, bras & paper, iron wrapped animal casing, aluminum, steel, alloys, plastic, silk, linen, gutta percha-rubber and zinc.

3. Primer: nickel, brass, copper, inside primed-benet, Martin primed or separate primed, pinfire and crispin.

4. Powder: black, semi-smokeless or smokeless

COLLECTING CATAGORIES

I have observed the following categories, however this aspect is mostly based upon the whims of the collector and are only limited by your interests and pocket book.

1. Military cartridges
2. Types of ignition
3. Automatic weapons ammunition
4. Rimfire
5. Paper & combustible
6. Packets or "by the box"
7. Shotgun shells
8. By headstamp
9. Rare cartridges only
10. By manufacturer

IDENTIFICATION

Looking at the lettering on the head or rim of the case can identify most cartridges. The lettering is applied with a die or so called head bunter, which is pressed into the metal of the case during manufacture. Other contributing factors are as follows.

1. The manufacturer initials or name that may also accompany the date and or caliber of the shell.
2. Monograms including raised lettering until the advent of revolvers.
3. Imprinted or "pressed into the metal" method.
4. Code systems such as DWM, RWS, G. Roth or other military manufacturers.
5. Type of primer, caliber, shape of the projectile, tactile markings or color codes.

CARTRIDGE MANUFACTURERS ORIGINATING FROM THE FOLLOWING 56 COUNTRIES OF INTEREST (PAST OR PRESENT) ARE LISTED OR REPRESENTED IN THIS GUIDE

Argentina
Australia
Austria
Belgium
Bulgaria
Burma
Brazil
Canada
Chile
China
Columbia
Cuba
Czechoslovakia
Denmark
Dominican Republic
Egypt
Ethiopia
Finland
France
Nazi Germany
Greece
Hungary
India
Indonesia
Iran
Iraq
Israel
Italy
Japan
Lebanon
Mexico
Morocco
Netherlands
Nigeria
North Korea
Norway
Peru
Poland
Portugal
Taiwan
Republic of South Africa
Romania
Saudi Arabia
South Korea
South Vietnam
Spain
Sudan
Sweden
Switzerland
Syria
Thailand
Turkey
United Kingdom
United States
USSR
Yugoslavia

ARGENTINA

Headstamp

C O A	(Monogram) Industrias Quimicus "Duperial", Buenos Aires	
F M C S F	Fabrica Militar de Cartuchos de San Francisco, San Francisco	
F M F L B	Fabrica Militar / Fray Luis Beltran, San Lorenzo	
F M S L	Fabrica Militar de Cartuchos de San Lorenzo, San Lorenzo	
FAMAP	Fabrica Argentina de Municiones de Armas Portatiles, San Larenzo	
FAMMAP	Fabrica Argentina de Militar de Municiones de Armas Portatiles, San Larenzo	
FMMAP B	Fabrica Militar de Municiones de Armas Portatiles, Borghi, San Larenzo	
FMMAP	Fabrica Militar de Municiones de Armas Portatiles	
I M P A	Industria Metallurgica y Plastica Argentina	
O R B E A	Cartucheria Orbea Argentina	
S P	Scorzato Hermanos Ltd., Lujan	

AUSTRALIA

Headstamp

M F	Small Arms Ammunition (Government) Factory No. 1, Footscray
M G	Small Arms Ammunition (Government) Factory No. 2, Footscray
M H	Small Arms Ammunition (Government) Factory No. 3, Hendon
M J	Small Arms Ammunition (Government) Factory No. 4, Hendon
M Q	Small Arms Ammunition (Government) Factory No. 5, Rocklea
M W	Small Arms Ammunition (Government) Factory No. 6, Welchpool
M S	Small Arms Ammunition (Government) Factory No 7, Salisbury

AUSTRIA

Headstamp

O J P	Oesterreichisches Jagdpatronenfabrik
H	Hirtenberger Zundhutchen und Patronenfabrik, Hirtenberg

BELGIUM

Headstamp

A E P	Anciens Etablissements Pieper, Herstal
C B / C R B	Cartoucherie Belge, Liege Cartoucherie Russo Belge, Liege
F N	Fabrique Nationale de Armes de Guerre, Herstal, Liege
VFM & CA	Capsulerie Leigoise, Francotte, May & Cie, Liege

BRAZIL

Headstamp

C B C	Companhia Brasiliera de Cartuchos, Sao Paulo
F C I	Fabrica de Cartuchos Itajuba, Minas Gerais
F R / R	Fabrica Realengo, Rio de Janeiro
D A M/MM	Directoria da Marinha (Navy) MM = Ministry of Marine

BULGARIA

Headstamp

V A F / 10	Durjava VoennA Fabrika, Kazanlak

BURMA

Headstamp

K P C	Government Arsenal, Rangoon, Pegu

1962 Feb

၁	၂	၃	၄	၅	၆	၇	၈	၉	၁၀
1	2	3	4	5	6	7	8	9	10

CANADA

Headstamp Canadian Industries Ltd.

Model 1910 Ross Rifle

D A	Dominion Arsenal, Quebec
D A C	Dominion Arsenal, Quebec
D A L	Dominion Arsenal, Lindsay, Ontario
D C	Dominion Cartridge Co., Montreal, Quebec
D C Co	Dominion Cartridge Co., Montreal, Quebec
D I	Defense Industries, Montreal, Quebec
F.W.L. Co.	F.W. Lamplough & Company, Montreal, Quebec
I V I	Industries Valcartier, Inc., Quebec
M M	Besa 7.92x57 machinegun / 9mm - sten gun 1942-45
R R Co	Ross Rifle Company, Montreal, Quebec
T R	Three Rivers (Dominion Rubber Munitions Ltd.), Three Rivers, Quebec
V C	Defense Industries, Verdun, Quebec

CHILE

Headstamp

F M E	Fabricas y Maestranzas del Ejercito, Santiago (F M G) (FAMAE)

CHINA

Headstamp   UK   US

11	Factory No. 11 Mundanjang
20	Factory No. 20
40	Factory No. 40
WCC	Western Cartridge Co. (7.92x57)

CHINA

Headstamp Peoples Republic of

C N I C	China North Industries Corporation, Beijing

11	351
31	352
41	391
51	501
61	601
71	641
81	651
101	661
111	671
121	911
171	944
201	946
211	947
215	948
221	964
301	6201
311	6202
312	6203
321	9121
341	9381

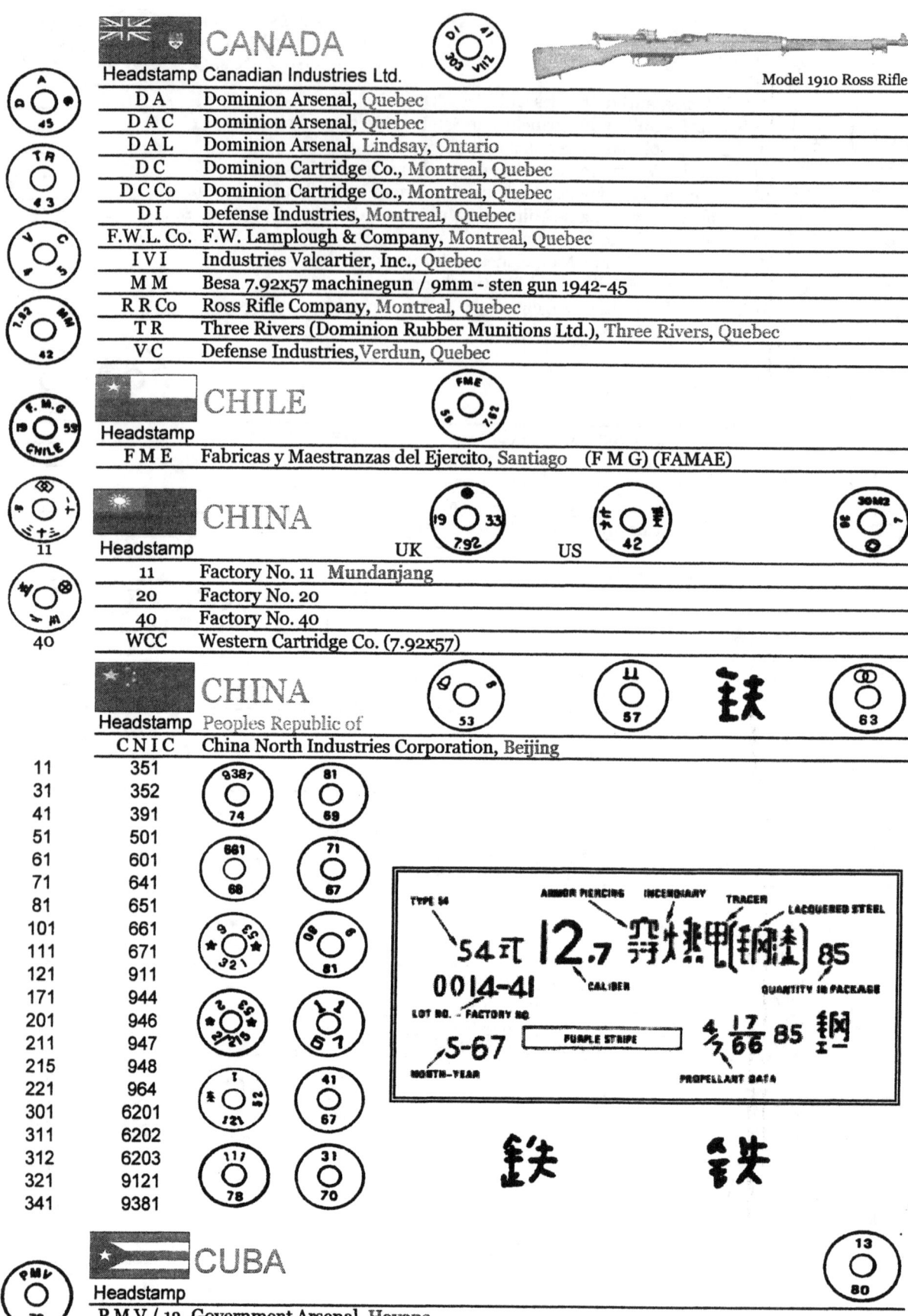

CUBA

Headstamp

P M V / 13	Government Arsenal, Havana

COLUMBIA

Headstamp

I M	Industria Militar, Bagota

CZECH...

Headstamp

P S	Povaske Strojarne, Povaska, Bystrica
S B / P	Sellier & Bellot, Prague (Praha)
Z / ZV(3B)	Cesklovenska Zbrojovka Akciova Spolecnost v Brne, Brno, Bystrica

DENMARK

Headstamp

Model 1895 Mannlicher Rifle

D R S	Dansk Rekylriffel Syndikat, Copenhagen
H A / A A	Haerens Ammunitionsarsenalet (Army Ammunition Arsenal), Copenhagen 1938-1950
H L	Haerens Krudtvaerk (Army Laboratorium), Copenhagen 1900-1937 -same as above-

DOMINICAN REPUBLIC

Headstamp

A C / R D	Armeria F.A. SC, San Cristobal

EGYPT

Headstamp

	Shoubra Arsenal, Cairo
١٠	State Factory No. 10
٢٧	State Factory No. 27

ETHIOPIA

FINLAND

Headstamp

S / S O	Suojeluskuntain se-je Konepa ja Oy (SAKO), Riihimaki
V M T	Valtion Metallitehtaat, Helsinki (VALMET)
V P T / P T	Valtion Patruunatehdas, Lapua

FRANCE

Headstamp

Model 86 Lebel Rifle

Metal Suppliers			
		A B S	Atelier de Construction de Bourges, Bourges
		A P	Establissements A. Pouvesle, Arcueil
		A P X	Atelier de Construction de Puteaux, Puteaux
B	PPC	A R S / R S	Atelier de Construction de Rennes, Rennes
BA	R	A T S / T S	Atelier de Construction de Tarbes, Tarbes
BDV	S	VIS	Atelier de Fabrication de Vincennes, Vincennes
BS	SD	B N	Parc d'Artillerie de Place de Besancon, Besancon
C	SF*	C F	Cartoucherie Francaise, Paris
CCM	TA	C N	Atelier Mechananique de Normandie, Normandy
CY	V	GEVELOT	Gevelot & Gaupillat Freres, Paris
D	A	G S F	Societe Francaise des Munitions, Issy - les - Moulineaux
FY	M	L M	Cartoucherie du Mans, Le Mans
D	N	M G	Marcel Gaupillat & Company, Paris
GP	AN	M I	Societe Meridionale d' Industrie, Marseille
H	L	M R	Manufacture de Machines du Haut-Rhin, Mulhouse-Bourtzwiller
HMB	F	R Y	Establissements Rey Freres, Nimes
HX		S F M / S F	Societe Francaise des Munitions, Issy - les - Moulineaux, Paris
I		T E	Cartoucherie de Toulouse, Toulouse
		T H	Trefeleries et Laminoirs du Havre, Le Havre
		V E	Cartoucherie de Valance, Valence
		V S	Parc d'Artillerie de Place de Verdun, Verdun

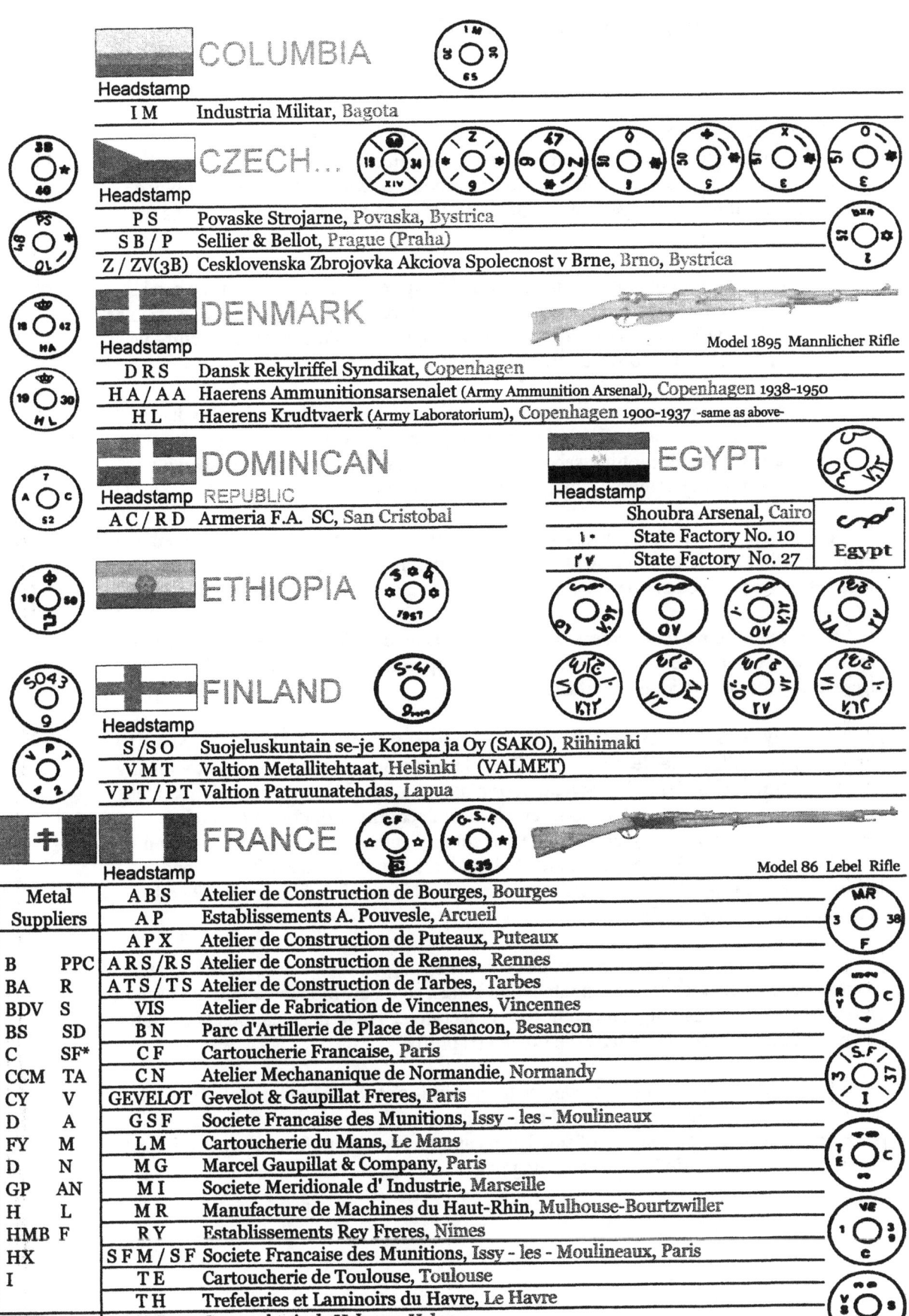

GERMAN CARTRIDGE CODES

The German Military authorities in 1934 devised a master plan of denoting all manufacturing facilities by a system of numeric codes. Each plant would be assigned a specific number to be marked on all headstamps produced from that facility combined with the last two digits of the year of manufacture. There were two distinct reasons for this system.

1. The first being the numerous and varied commercial symbols or trade marks which would identify the manufacturer, however with some companies such as RWS or DWM operating 20 or more plants, who could say which facility was responsible for a specific batch or shipment.

2. The second reason was the need to disguise the manufacturer location in the event that an enemy captured its product in time of war. This would hopefully prevent plans of plotting sabotage by mapping out the industrial dispersion to determine raw material supply routes and railway traffic.

For a short period of two years, even the year of manufacturer was designated by a capital letter that was later abolished because the apparent confusion outweighed its benefit. However the codes that were used for those years (K) = 1934 (G) or (S) = 1935

The plan to move to a numeric system went ahead as scheduled but the assigned number would be preceded by a capital (P), which represents the German word Patronenfabriken or cartridge manufacturer.

On July 1, 1940 A revised designation plan went into effect that introduced a 1 to 3 uncapitalized alphabetical letter system. These letters are in no way consistent with any previous commercial trademark designation or plant location. The letters are deliberately garbled and uncapitalized as to not show any logical decoding order or pattern of consistency. Only three manufacturers failed to comply and used capital letters, which were (BK), (BT) and (CA), and only Hugo Schneider, Leipzig, Sachsen (P-181) and Markisches Walzwerke, Stausberg, Bez- Potsdam (P-315) continued to use the P code system until the spring of 1941.

The third and final revision took place in the spring of 1945 after it was known that some code directories had fallen into allied hands, so a new alphabetical letter system was assigned to the remaining ammunition manufacturers. These designations were in the latter part of the alphabet, especially the (s) and (t) prefix.

Small arms manufacturers as well as large munitions manufacturers also used the letter code system on gun parts and shell case headstamps, but our interests in this guide remain only to explore the identity of small arms ammunition manufacturers of which 84 of them have been identified in the following pages.

GERMANY

Occupied - Austria, Czechoslovakia, France, Hungary, Poland, Romania

Ammunition Manufacturers — Model 98 Mauser Rifle

(P) Code	(L) Code	Manufacturer
-	aan	Mitteldeutsche Metallwarenfabrik, Glauchau, Saxony
P-244	ab	Mundlos Nahmaschinenfabrik, Madgeburg-Neustadt
P-480	ac	Carl Walther Waffenfabrik, Zella-Mehlis, Thuringia
P-69	ad	Patronen-Zundhutchen und Metallwarenfabrik, Shoenbeck
-	afu	August Winkhaus, Muenster
-	ajn	Union Sprengstoff und Zundmittel Werke, Alt-Beron
P-90D	ak	Munitionsfabriken, Sellior & Bellot, Vlasim, (Czechoslovakia)
-	akv	Berg und Huettenwerksgesellschaft, Radotin, Prague, (Czechoslovakia)
P-635	am	Gustloff-Werke Otto Eberhardt Patronenfabrik, Hirtenberg, Niederdonau, (Austria)
	ama	Herdfabrik Imperial, Buende, Westfalen
	an	C. Beuttenmuller & Cie Metallwarenfabrik, Bretten, Baden
	anz	Machinen und Armaturenfabrik, Madgeburg
	aqt	Otto Grusen und Company, Magdeburg
P-243	ar	Mauser-Werke, Berlin-Borsigwalde
P-131	asb	Deutsche Waffen und Munitionsfabriken, Berlin-Borsigwalde
P-58	asf	Graetz Lampen und Metallwarenfabrik, Berlin
P-382	asr	Hanseatische Kettenwerk (HAK), Hamburg, Schleswig-Holstein
P-155	asw	E.F. Horster, Stahl-u. Metallwarenfabrik, Solingen
P-456	aue	Metall und Eisen, Nurnberg
P-270	auf	Metal Guss u. Presswerke H. Deihl, Nurnberg
-	auu	Patronenhulsen und Metallwarenfabrik, Rokycany, Pilsen (Czechoslovakia)
P	aux	Polte Armaturen und Machinenfabrik, Madgeburg, Sachsen
P-154	auy	Polte Armaturen und Machinenfabrik, Gruneburg, Nordbahn, (Poland)
-	auz	Polte Armaturen und Machinenfabrik, Arnstadt, Thuringia
-	av	Vereinigte Deutsche Metallwerke, Werdohl
-	avk	Ruhrstahl, Brackwede-Bielefeld
P-414	avt	Silva Metallwerke, Madgeberg-Neustadt
P-345	avu	Silva Metallwerke, Genthin
P-222	awl	Union-Gesellschaft fuer Metallindustrie, Sils Van de Loo & Co. Werl-Frondenberg, Ruhr
P-152	awt	Wurtembergische Metallwarenfabrik, Geislingen, Steige, Wurttemberg
-	axq	Erfurter Laden Industrie, Erfurt
-	axs	Berndorfer Metallwarenfabrik, Amstettin (Austria)
-	ay	Alois Pirkl Elektrotechn Fabrik, Reichenberg, Sudetenland
P-27	ayf	Erma, B.Geipel, Waffenfabrik, Erfurt, Thuringia
-	ba	Sundwiger Messingwerke, Iserlohn, Westfalen
-	bb	A. Laue & Company, Berlin
-	bc	Kupfer und Messingwerke, Langenberg, Rheinland
	bd	Metallwerke Fa. Lange, Bodenbach, Sudetenland (Czechoslovakia)
	be	Berndorfer Warenfabrik, Berndorf, Niederdonau, (Austria)
	bf	Deutsche Rohrenwerke, Mulheim, Rheinland
-	bg	Boehler & Company, Zweigniederlassung Edelstahlwerke, Berlin
-	bj	Niebecker und Schumacher, Iserlohn, Westfalen
-	bk	Metall- Walz und Plattierwarenfabrik, Wupertal
-	blu	Sprengstoffwerke Blamau, Felixdorf
-	bmv	Rheinmetall-Borsig, Sommerda, Thuringia
-	bnd	Maschinenfabrik, Augsburg, Nurnberg
P-207	bne	Metallwerke Odertal, Odertal
P-186	bnf	Metalwerke Wolfenbuttel, Wulfenbuttel
P-452	bnr	Fr. Drabert Sohne Machinenfabrik, Minden, Westfalen
P-660	bnz	Steyr Daimler Puch, Steyr, (Austria)
P-963	bpr	Johannes Grossfuss Metal & Locierwarenfabriik, Dobeln, Sachsen
-	bt	Radiowerke Horny, Wien
P-400	bwa	Gebruder Gabler Fingerhutz und Metallwarenfabrik, Schorndorf, Wurtemberg
-	byc	Aug. Klonne, Bruckenbauanstalt, Dortmund
P-42	byf	Mauser Werke, Oberndorf am Neckar, Wurttemberg
P-75	byw	Johannes Schafer, Stettiner Schraubenwerke, Stettin, Pomerania

MP-40 SMG

GERMANY
Occupied - Austria, Czechoslovakia, France, Hungary, Poland, Romania -

(P) Code	(L) Code	Ammunition Manufacturers
P-147	ce	J.P. Sauer und Sohn Gewehrfabrik, Suhl, Thuringia
P-287	can	A. Wallmeyer Machinenfabrik, Eisenach, Thuringia
P-398	cdo	Theodore Bergmann & Co., Waffen und Munitionsfabriken, Velten, Berlin
Pcdp	cdp	Theodore Bergmann & Co., Waffen und Munitionsfabriken, Bernau, Berlin
-	cf	Westfalische Anhaltische Sprengstoff, Oranienburg, Brandenburg
P-249	cg	Finower Industrie, Finow/Mark, Brandenburg
-	cgt	Josef Stefshy, Stockerau, Niederdonau
-	ch	Fabrique National d'armes d'querra, Herstal & Liege (Belgium)
P-239	clc	A. Richard Herder Stahlwaren und Werkezeugfabrik, Solingen
P-64	cnx	Gustav Appel Machinenfabrik, Berlin
P-175	cof	Carl Eickhorn Waffenfabrik, Solingen, Westfalen
P-176	crs	Paul Weyersberg und Co., Waffenfabrik, Solingen, Westfalen
P-238	csd	Durkoppwerke, Bielefeld
P-178	csr	Gebruder Heller, Thuringia
-	cts	Markisches Werke, Forge, Halver
P-174	cvl	WKC Waffenfabrik, Solingen-Wald
-	cwg	Westfalische Anhaltische Sprengstoff, Coswig
-	cxm	Gustav Genshow & Co., Berlin
-	czo	Heeres-Zeugamt, Geschosswerkstatt, Konnigsberg, East Prussia
P-224	czs	Brennabor Werke, Brandenburg
-	dbg	Dynamit, Duneberg
-	dgl	Remo Gewehrfabrik, Gerbruder Rempt, Suhl, Thuringia
-	dma	Heeres-Munitionsanstalt und Geschosswerkstatt, Zeithain
P-151	dnf	RWS Rheinisch-Westfalische Sprengstoff, Nurnberg & Stadeln, Bavaria
P-405	dnh	Dynamit, Durlach, Baden
P-316	dom	Westfalische Metallindustrie, Lippstadt
P-945	dot	Waffenwerke Brunn, Brunn, (Czechoslovakia)
P-14A	dou	Waffenwerke Brunn, Povazska & Bystrica (Czechoslovakia)
-	drv	Hasag Eisen und metallwerke, Tschenstochau (Czechoslovakia)
-	dut	Spinnfleugelfabrik, Neudorf
P-237	duv	Berlin-Lubecker Maschinenfabrik, Lubeck, Schleswig-Holstein
-	dve	Adolf Knoch, Saalfeld
-	dwm	Liefergemeinschaft Dornbirn, Ludwig Rigger, Dornbirn
P757	dyu	Heinrich Huppman Maschinenfabrik, Kitzgen-Etwashausen
-	dza	Bleiwerke, Hamberg & Wilhelmsburg
P-379	eba	Metallwarenfabriken Scharfenberg & Teubert, Breitungen-Werra, Thuringia
P-413	edq	Deutche Waffen- und Munitionsfabriken, Lubeck & Schultup
P-327	eds	Zuendappwerke, Nuernberg
-	eeh	F. Soennecker, Bonn
P-315	eej	Markisches Walzwerke, Stausberg, Bez- Potsdam
-	eem	Selve Kronbiegel, Dornheim & Sommerda
-	eeo	Deutche Waffen- und Munitionsfabriken, Posen, West Prussia
P-198	eey	Metallwarenfabrik Truenbrietzen, Roederhof
P-120	emp	Dynamit, Alfred Nobel, Empelde, Hanover
P-346	eom	H. Huck Metallwarenfabrik, Nurnberg, Bavaria
-	evz	Bergbau, Salzgitter
P-423	exq	Clemens Kreher Metall-Blechspielwaren-u. Trommelfabrik, Marienberg
-	exw	Metallwerke Holleischen, Sudetenland
P-28	faa	Deutche Wafen- und Munitionsfabriken, Karlsruhe
P-334	fb	Mansfield, Rothenberg/Saale
-	fde	Dynamit, Foerde
P-491	fer	Metallwerke Wandhofen, Schwerte
-	feu	Krone Presswerke, Berlin
P-240	ffc	Friedrich Herder Stahlwarenfabrik, Solingen
P-416	flp	Heintze & Blankertz, Erste Dutsche Stahlfederfabrik, Werk Oranienburg, Berlin
P-359	foy	Horn Tachometerfabrik, Leipzig

Occupied - Austria, Czechoslovakia, France, Hungary, Poland, Romania -

GERMANY
Ammunition Manufacturers

Sturmgewehr 44

(P) Code	(L) Code	Manufacturer
P-457	fpo	H. Meinecke, Breslau
P-208	fsa	Federstahl, Kassel
P-132	fva	Draht- und Metallwarenfabrik, Salzwedel, Sachsen
P-122	fxo	C.G. Haenel Waffen und Fahrradfabrik, Suhl, Thuringia
	ga	Hirsch Kupfer- und Messingwerke, Finow/Mark
	ghf	Fritz Kiess und Company Waffenfabrik, Suhl
	gsc	S. A. Belge de Mecanique et de le Armament, Mecar, Monceau-sur-sambre (Belgium)
	guy	Werkzeugmaschinenfabrik Oerlikon, Buhrle & Co., Zurich, (Switzerland)
-	ham	Dynamit, Hamm
P-169	has	Pulverfabrik Hasloch, Hasloch-am-main
P-340	hhw	Metallwerke Silberhutte, St. Andreasberg/Harz
-	hhx	M. Boehme, Grosshartmannsdorf, Sachsen
-	hhy	Louis Ulbricht, Rosenthal, Erzgebirge
P-25	hla	Metallwarenfabrik Treuenbrietzen, Sebaldushof
P-163	hlb	Metallwarenfabrik Treuenbrietzen, Selterhof
P-442	hlc	Zieh- und Stazwerke, Schleusingen
P-198	hld	Metallwerke Treuenbrietzen, Belsig/Mark, Brandenburg
-	hle	Metallwerke Treuenbrietzen, Roederhof
-	hrk	Schluermann und Company, Westfalen
P-162	hrn	Presswerk, Metgethen, East Prussia
P-185	i	Astra Werke, Chemnitz, Sachsen
P-265	ja	R. und G. Schmole Metallwerke, Menden, Westfalen
-	jkg	Koenig Staatliche Eisen Stahl-und Maschinenfabrik, Budapest, Hungary
-	jry	Hermann Herthold, Olbernhau, Sudetenland, (Czechoslovakia)
-	jtb	S. A. Tavaro, Geneva, (Switzerland)
-	jua	Danuvia Waffen und Munitionsfabriken, Budapest, (Hungary)
	kam	Hasag Eisen und Metallwerke, Skarzysko - Kamienna (Poland)
	keb	Jiranek und Company, Brunn
	kfa	Statliches (Sarajevo State Arsenal), Sarajevo (Yugoslovia)
	kfk	Dansk Rekylriffl Syndicat, Copenhagen, (Denmark)
-	krl	Dynamit, Afred Nobel Co., Kruemmel, Bez-Koblenz
-	kry	Lignose Sprengstoffwerke, Kruppamuhle
-	ksb	Manufacture National d' Armes de Lavallois, Paris (France)
-	lkm	Sellier & Bellot Munitionsfabriken, Praha (Praque) (Czechoslovakia)
-	na	Westfalische Kupfer- und Messingwerke, Ludenscheid, Westfalen
-	nbe	Hasag Eisen und Metallwerke, Apparatbau Tschenstochau (Poland)
-	ndn	Heinrich Bluecher, Fabrik technic Buersten, Spremberg
-	nfx	RWS Munitionsfabrik, Warsaw, (Poland) & Praque, (Czechoslovakia)
-	nhr	Rheinmetall-Borsig, Sommerda, Thuringia
	nrh	Johannsen und Zieger, Oranienburg
	oxo	Teuto Metallwerke, Osnabruck, Hannover
	oyj	Alteliers de Construction de Tarbes, Tarbes (France)
	pjj	Haerens Ammunitionsarsenalet, Copenhagen, (Denmark)
-	qa	William Prym, Stollberg, Rheinland
-	qrb	Sezione del Pirotechico, Bologna (Italy)
-	r	Westfalische Anhaltisch Sprengstoff, Reinsdorf
-	ra	Deutsches Messingwerke C. Eveking, Berlin-Niederschoneweide
P-168	rtl	Pulverfabrik, Koln-Rottweil
-	s	Dynamit, Alfred Nobel, Werke Lumbrays
-	skd	Selve Kronbriegel, Dornheim, Suhl
-	suk	Deusche Waffen u. Munitionsfabriken, Karlsruhe-Durlach
P-42	svw	Mauser Werke, Oberndorf am Neckar, Wurttemburg (supplemental components P-s42)
P-959	swp	Mauserwerke (Waffenwerke Brunn), Brunn, Brno, (Czechoslovakia)
P-160	t	Dynamit, Alfred Nobel, Troisdorf, Rheinland
-	ta	Duerener Metallwerke, Berlin
-	ua	Osnabrucker Kupfer- und Drahtwerke, Osnbruck, Hannover

GERMANY

Occupied - Austria, Czechoslovakia, France, Hungary, Poland, Romania -

MP-18

(P) Code	(L) Code	**Ammunition** Manufacturers
P-67	unt	H. Unttendorfer, Munitionsfabrik, Nuremberg, Bayern
P-94	va	Kabel- und Metallwerke Neumeyer, Nurnberg, Bavaria
P-181	wa	Hugo Schneider, Lampenfabrik, Leipzig, Sachsen
P-128	wal	Wolf & Co. Walsrode, Hannover
P-370	wb	Hugo Schneider, Berlin, Kopenick
P-797	wc	Hugo Schneider, Meuselwitz, Thuringia
-	wd	Hugo Schneider, Taucha, Sachsen
-	we	Hugo Schneider, Langeweissen, Thuringia
-	wf	Hugo Schneider, Hasag Eisen und Metallwerke, Kielce (Poland)
P-490	wg	Hugo Schneider, Altenberg, Thuringia
-	wh	Hugo Schneider, Eisenach, Thuringia
-	wj	Hugo Schneider, Oberweissbach, Thuringia
-	wk	Hugo Schneider, Schlieben, Sachsen-Anhalt
-	wn	Hugo Schneider, Dernbach, Thuringia
-	xa	Busch-Jager, Ludenschneider Metallwerke, Ludenscheid
-	y	Jagpatronen, Zundhutchen u. Metallwarenfabrik, Budapest (Hungary)
-	ya	Saechsische Metallwarenfabrik, August Wellner & Sohn, Aue in Sachsen
-	zb	Kupferwerk Ilsenberg, Ilsenberg, Harz

Signal-Flare - Pyrotechnic Manufacturers

aj	Soerensen und Koester, Neumuenster
al	Deutsche Leucht-und Signalmittelwerke, Dr. Feistel, Berlin-Charlottenburg
ap	Deutsche Leucht-und Signalmittelwerke, Dr. Feistel, Wuppertal, Ronsdorf, Rheinland
asb*	Deutsche Waffen und Munitionsfabriken, Berlin-Borsigwalde
auj	Monheimer Ketten und Metallwaren-Industrie Poetz und Sand, Monheim-Dusseldorf
bqt	Pirotechnische Fabrik Eugen Miller, Vienna, (Austria)
bvv	Rothmueller-Mewa, Wien
cbl	Vereinigte Deutsche Metallwerke, Nuremberg West
dye	Erst Alpenlandische Pyrotechnik, Ed Pitschamann und Co., Innsbruck, (Austria)
eca	Oscar Fischer, Baden
ecc	Pyrotechnische Fabrik, Mohringen
ecd	Earl Lippold Pyrotechnische Fabrik, Wuppertal-Elderfield, Rheinland
edg	Henckels Zwillingswerke, Solingen
fnk	Adolf Hopf, Tambach-Dietharz, Thuringia
gtb	J.F. Eisfeld und Pyrotechnische Fabriken, Guntersberg
hgs	W. C. Gustav Burmeister Pyrotechnische Fabrik und Signalmittelwerke, Hamburg
kfg	Gesellschaft zur Verwertung chemischer Erzeugnisse, Kaufering
kls	Styer Daimler Puch, Warsaw (Poland)
kum	Hartmann und Braun, Frankfurt am-main
kun	J.F. Eisfeld Pulver und Pyrotechnische Fabriken, Kunigunde
ldb	Deutsche Pyrotechnische Fabriken, Malchow, Mecklenburg
ldc	Deutsche Pyrotechnische Fabriken, Cleebron, Wurtemburg
ldn	Deutsche Pyrotechnische Fabriken, Neumarkt, Schlesien

Pre-Code German Headstamps

D / G E C O	Gustav Genchow & Company, Berlin / Durlach
D M / DMK	Deutsche Metallpatronenfabrik, Karlsruhe
D W A	Deutsche Werke Actiengesellschaft, Spandau /Berlin
D W M	Deutsche Waffen und Munitionsfabriken, Karlsruhe
G C D	G. C. Dornheim, Suhl
G R	G. Roth, Wien und Pressburg
MW / MWS	Munitionswerke, Shoenbeck-am-elbe
P & S	Potz & Sand, Mulheim
P.	Polte, Madgeburg
R M S	Rheinische Metallwaren und Maschinenfabrik, Sommerda
R W S / N	Rheinische Westfalische Sprengstoff, Nurnberg
S	Koenigliche Munitionsfabrik, Spandau
S B	Sellior & Bellot, Schoenbeck
S E	Staatliche, Erfurt
S K D	Selve - Kronbiegel - Dornheim, Suhl
S. E	Munitionsfabrik Stettin, Stettin, Prussia

 Note: P-Code or (*) marked entries also produced ammunition

GERMANY

Infantry Luger

Small Arms Manufacturers until 1945

(P) Code	(L) Code	Manufacturer
-	aak	Waffenfabrik Brunn, Prague, (Czechoslovakia)
P-480	ac	Carl Walther Waffenfabrik, Zella-Mehlis, Thuringia
P-69	ad	Patronen-Zundhutchen und Metallwarenfabrik, Shoenbeck an der elbe, Sachsen
-	aek	F. Dusek Waffenzeugung, Opoczno Bei Nashod, (Poland)
	ai	Unknown
-	ajf	Junker und Ruh, Karlsrue, Baden
-	an	C. Beutemueller und Company Metallwarenfabrik, Bretten-Baden
P-131	asb	Deutsche Waffen und Munitionsfabriken, Berlin, Borsigwalde
P-154	auy	Polte Armaturen und Maschinenfabrik, Arsnstadt, Thuringia
-	avk*	Ruhrstahl, Brackwede-Bielefeld
P-152	awt	Wurtembergische Metallwarenfabrik, Geislingen, Steige, Wurttemberg
P-27	ayf	Erma, B.Geipel, Waffenfabrik, Erfurt, Thuringia
-	azg	Siemens-Schuckert Werke, Berlin
	bcd	Wilhelm Gusstloff Werke, Weimar, Thuringia
	bh	Waffenfabrik Brunn, Povaszka, Bystrica, (Czechoslovakia)
	bkp	Roehrenwerk Johannes Surman, Arnesberg
	bky	Bohmische Waffenfabrik, von Prague, Werk ung-Brod, Moravia, (Czechoslovakia)
-	blp	Grazer Maschinen und Waggonbaufabrik, Graz
P-660	bnz	Steyr Daimler Puch, Steyr, (Austria)
P-963	bpr	Johannes Grossfuss Metal und Locierwarenfabrik, Bobeln, Sachsen
-	bt*	Radiowerk Horny, Wien
P-42	byf	Mauser Werke, Oberndorf am Neckar, Wurttemberg
-	bys	Ruhrstahl,Guss-stahlwerke, Witten
-	bzt	Fritz Wolf Gewehrfabrik, Zella-Mehlis, Thuringia
P-147	ce	J.P. Sauer und Sohn Gewehrfabrik, Suhl, Thuringia
-	cnd	National Krupp Registrierkassen, Berlin
P-175	cof	Carl Eickhorn Waffenfabrik, Solingen, Westfalen
-	con	Franz Stock Madchinen und Werkzeugfabrik, Berlin
-	cos	Merz Werke, Gerbruder Merz, Frankfurt am main, Hessen-Nassua
-	cpj	Havelwerke, Brandenburg
-	cpo	Rheinmetall-Borsig, Berlin, Marienfeld
-	ch*	Fabrique Nationale d' Armes de Guerre, Herstal, Liege, (Belgium)
-	cr	Zander und optiz, Berlin
P-176	crs	Paul Weyersberg und Co., Waffenfabrik, Solingen, Westfalen
P-174	cvl	WKC Waffenfabrik, Solingen-Wald
-	cyq	Spreewerke, Metallwarenfabrik, Berlin-Spandau
-	cyw	Saechische Guss-stahlwerke Doehlen, Sachsen
-	dfb	Whilhelm Gustloff Werke, Suhl, Thuringia
-	dgl*	Remo Gewehrfabrik, Gebruder Rempt, Suhl, Thuringia
P-945	dot	Waffenwerke Brunn, Brunn, (Czechoslovakia)
P-14A	dou	Waffenwerke Brunn, Bystrica, (Czechoslovakia)
-	dov	Waffenwerke Brunn, Wsetin, (Czechoslovakia)
-	dox	Waffenfabrik Brunn, Podbrezova, (Czechoslovakia)
P-237	duv	Berlin-Lubecker Maschinenfabrik, Lubeck, Schleswig-Holstein
	eeg	Herman Weihrauch, Gewhr und Fahrradteilfabriken, Zella-Mehlis, Thuringia
-	eeo*	Deutsche Waffen- und Munitionsfabriken, Posen, West Prussia
-	eun	Rana-Werke, Klardorf, Oberpfalz
-	fa	Mansfeld, Hettstedt, Sud/Harz, Sachsen-Anhalt
-	fnh	Bohmische Waffenfabrik, Prague, Strakonitz, (Czechoslovakia)
-	fwh	Norddeursche Machinenfabrik, Hauptverwaltung, Berlin
P-122	fxo	C.G. Haenel Waffen und Fahrradfabrik, Suhl, Thuringia
-	fze	F.W. Holler Waffenfabrik, Solingen, Westfalen
-	fzs	Heinrich Krieghoff Waffenfabrik, Suhl, Thuringia
-	gal	Wagner und Company, Muehlhausen, Thuringia
-	gpt	Gustav Bittner, Weipert, Sudetengau

Note: P-Code or (*) marked entries also produced ammunition

GERMANY

Navy Luger

Small Arms Manufacturers until 1945

(P) Code	(L) Code	
-	gqm	Loch und Hartenberger, Idar-Oberstein
-	hta	Koenig und Company, Wein
-	jhv	Metallwaren, Waffen und Maschinenfabrik, Budapest, (Hungary)
-	jwa	Manufacture de armes Chatellerfault, Chatellerfault, (France)
-	kfk*	Dansk Rekylriffel Syndicat, Copenhagen, (Denmark)
-	kur	Steyr Daimler Puch, Furhofstrasse, Graz, (Austria)
-	kwm	S. A. Fiat, Turin, (Italy)
-	kye	Fabrica de Armamant Brascow, Brascow, (Romania)
-	kyn	Armament et Munitiuni, Brasow, (Romania)
-	moc	Johann Springers Erbrn Gewehrfabrikanten, Vienna, (Austria)
-	nea	Walther Steiner Eisenkonstruktionen, Suhl, Thuringia
-	nec	Waffenwerke Brunn, Werk Gurein, Prague, (Czechoslovakia)
-	pla	Unknown
-	qlv	Unknown
-	qnw	Unknown
-	qve	Carl Walther Waffenfabrik, Zella-Mehlis, Thuringia
-	rde	Unknown
P-42	svw	Mauser Werke, Oberndorf am Neckar, Wurttemburg (supplemental components P-s42)
P-959	swp	Mauserwerke (Waffenwerke Brunn), Brunn, Brno, (Czechoslovakia)
-	tjk	Unknown
-	tpk	Unknown
-	tpn	Unknown
-	tvw	Unknown

Note: P-Code or (*) marked entries also produced small arms ammunition

Large Caliber Manufacturers

(P) Code	(L) Code	
-	amp	Dortmund Hoerder Huettenverein, Dortmund
P	aux	Polte Armaturen und Maschinenfabrik, Madgeburg, Sachsen
	bcd	Wilhelm Gustloff Werke, Weimar, Thuringia
	bmv*	Rheinmetall-Borsig, Sommerda, Thuringia
	bwo	Rheinmetall-Borsig, Dusseldorf, Westfalen
	bwp	Berlin Anhaltische Maschinenbau, Dessau
	bxb	Skoda Werke, Pilsen, (Czechoslovakia)
	bxe	Bochumer Verein fur Guss-stahlfabrikation, Bochum
	bxm	Vereinigte Zuender und Kabelwerke, Meissen
	bye	Hannoversche Maschinenbau, Hanover
	cpo	Rheinmetall-Borsig, Berlin
	cpp	Rheinmetall-Borsig, Guben Werke, Brandenburg
	cpq	Rheinmetall-Borsig, Breslau, Silesia
	dsh	Waffenwerke Inc. F. Jancek, Gewehrwerke, Prague-Nulse, (Czechoslovakia)
	ebk	Machinenbau und Bahnbedarf, Spandau, Babelsberg
	exp	Landes-Lieferungsgenossenscaft des Tischlerhandwerks, Bezirk, Westfalen
	eyd	Heidenreich und Harbeck, Hamburg
	feh	Machinenfabrik Donauwoerth, Donauwoerth
	gsb	Rheinmetall-Borsig (Des Ateliers De La Dyle), Louvain, (Belgium)
	guy*	Werkzeugmaschinenfabrik Oerlikon, Buhrle und Company, Zurich, (Switzerland)
	hew	Waffenfabrik Inc. F. Jancek, Pangrac, (Czeckoslovakia)
	hhg	Rheinmetall-Borsig, Berlin-Tegel
	kfk*	Dansk Rekylriffel Syndicat, Kopenhagen, (Denmark)
	mpr	Hispano Suiza, Geneva (Switzerland)
	mrb	Aktiengesellschaft Skoda Werke, Prague-Smichow, (Czechoslovakia)
	myx	Rheinmetall-Borsig, Sommerda, Thuringia
	nhr*	Rheinmetall-Borsig, Sommerda, Thuringia
	nyv	Rheinmetall-Borsig, Unterluess, Hanover
	pmu	Unknown

GREECE

Headstamp

E K / E N K	Greek Powder and Cartridge Co., Athens (German contract) (PCH=French contract)
P C H	Poudres (Powder) Carttoucherie (Cartridge) Hellenique (Greek) Co., Athens

HUNGARY

Headstamp

ꓘ A H	Csepel Arsenal, Budapest	
D M	Danuvia Munitionsfabrik, Budapest	
F.GY. BP.	Fehyvergyar Budapest, Budapest	Psz GZS
M L / 23	Magyar Loszermuvek RT, Veszprem	
M F / 21	Matravideki Femmuvek, Sirok	

INDIA

Headstamp

smle #1 mk III Royal Enfield Rifle

D F	Dum Dum Arsenal, Dum Dum, (Bengal) (Now Calcutta)	DI NI SI
K F	Kirkee Arsenal, Kirkee, (Bombay) (Now Maharahtra)	
K H	Khamaria Arsenal, Jubbulpore, (Central Provinces) (Now Madhya Pradesh)	
O F V	Varangaon Arsenal, Bhusawal	

INDONESIA

Headstamp

A D	Angkatan Darat, (PSM) Turen, Maland, East Java
P S M	Pabrik Senjasta Mesiu, Turen, Maland, East Java

IRAN

1951-1968   1960   1968   1970

Arabic	Number
۱	1
۲	2
۳	3
٤	4
٥	5
٦	6
۷	7
۸	8
۹	9
٠	0

خارق	AP
عاربة	Ball
باسة	Cartridge
مصر	Egypt
جم	Grams
حارق	Incendiary
ملم	Millimeters
کا رصاص لیلي	Night tracer
کا رصاص	Tracer
٥٤ × ٧.٦٢	7.62x54R
۹	9x19

IRAQ

1949   1949   1961   1964

-۲-۳۲

ISRAEL

Headstamp

I M I / T Z	Israeli Military Industries, Tel Aviv	TZ / TZZ - Taasiya Tsviat
T A	Tel Aviv Arsenal (Israeli Military Industries), Tel Aviv	(9mm export only)
A E = (E A)	Eretz Ayalon, Rehovot (Private "underground factory" Pre-Independence 1948)	

ITALY

Headstamp

B	Pirotechnia di Bologna, Bologna
B P D	Brombrini Parodi Defino, Rome - (AOC) contract for Egypt
C / P E C	Pirotechnia di Capua, Capua
G F L	Giulio Fiocchi, Lecco
L B C	Leon Beaux & Company, Milan
M / M C M	Munizioni e Cartucce Martignoni, Genoa
S M I/S Y I	Societa Metallurgica Italiana, Campo Tizzore (C T)
	A.A.- C.A.- L.N. or T.M. at the 12 o'clock element position are chief inspector initials

Model 38 Carcano

JAPAN

Headstamp

None	Imperial Japanese Army Arsenal, Tokyo
ア	Aichi Naval Arsenal, Aichi
ト	Toyokawa Naval Arsenal, Tokyo
H	Hokuto Shinto Kabushiki Co.
ヨ	Yokosuka Naval Arsenal, Yokosuka
K	Kynoch, England 1916 contract
J-AO (A)	Asahi Okuma Arms Corporation, Asahi
J- CH	Chuo Kayaku Kako Kaisha Co.
J- S T	Showa-Kayaku, Inc. , Tsuruoka
J-T E / T E	Toyo Seiki Manufacturing, Company, Ltd., Tokyo

Nambu

Model 99 Arisaka Rifle

11 mm Murata

MEXICO

Headstamp

C D M	Cartuchos Deportivos de Mexico, Cuernavaca, Morelos
F DE M	Fabrica Nacional de Municiones, Sante Fe
F M	Fabrica Nacional de Municiones, Sante Fe
F N C M	Fabrica Nacional de Cartuchos e Municoes, Sao Paulo

MOROCCO

Headstamp

M N A M	Manufacture National d'Armes et de Munitions, Casablanca

NEPAL

Headstamp

M F S	Munitions Factory, Sundari

NETHERLANDS

Headstamp

A I	Artillerie Inrichtingen, Zandam
D o	Hirtenberg Patronenfabrik, Dordrecht
N W M	Nederlandsche Wapen en Munitiefabriek, 's Hertogenbosch, North Brabant

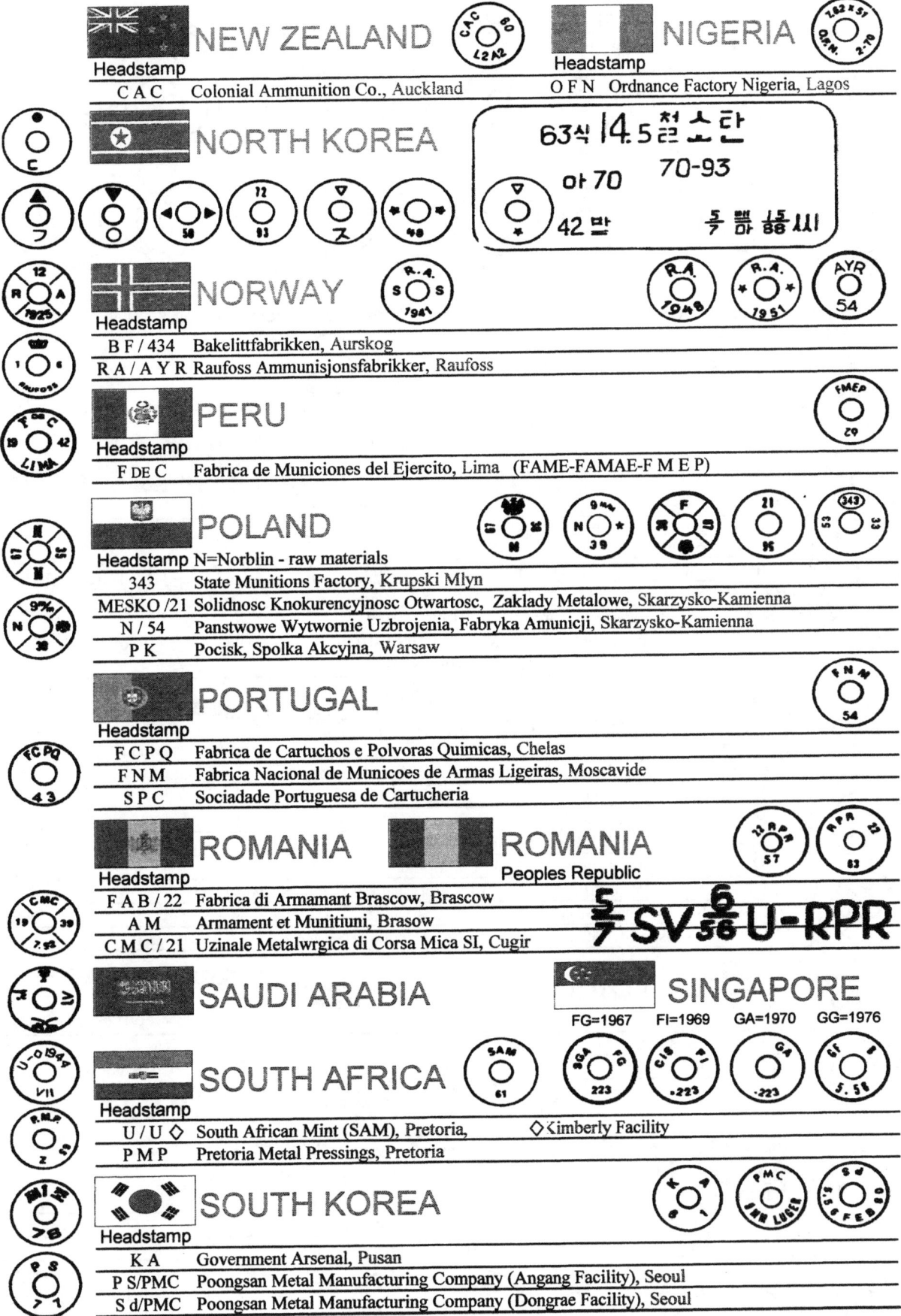

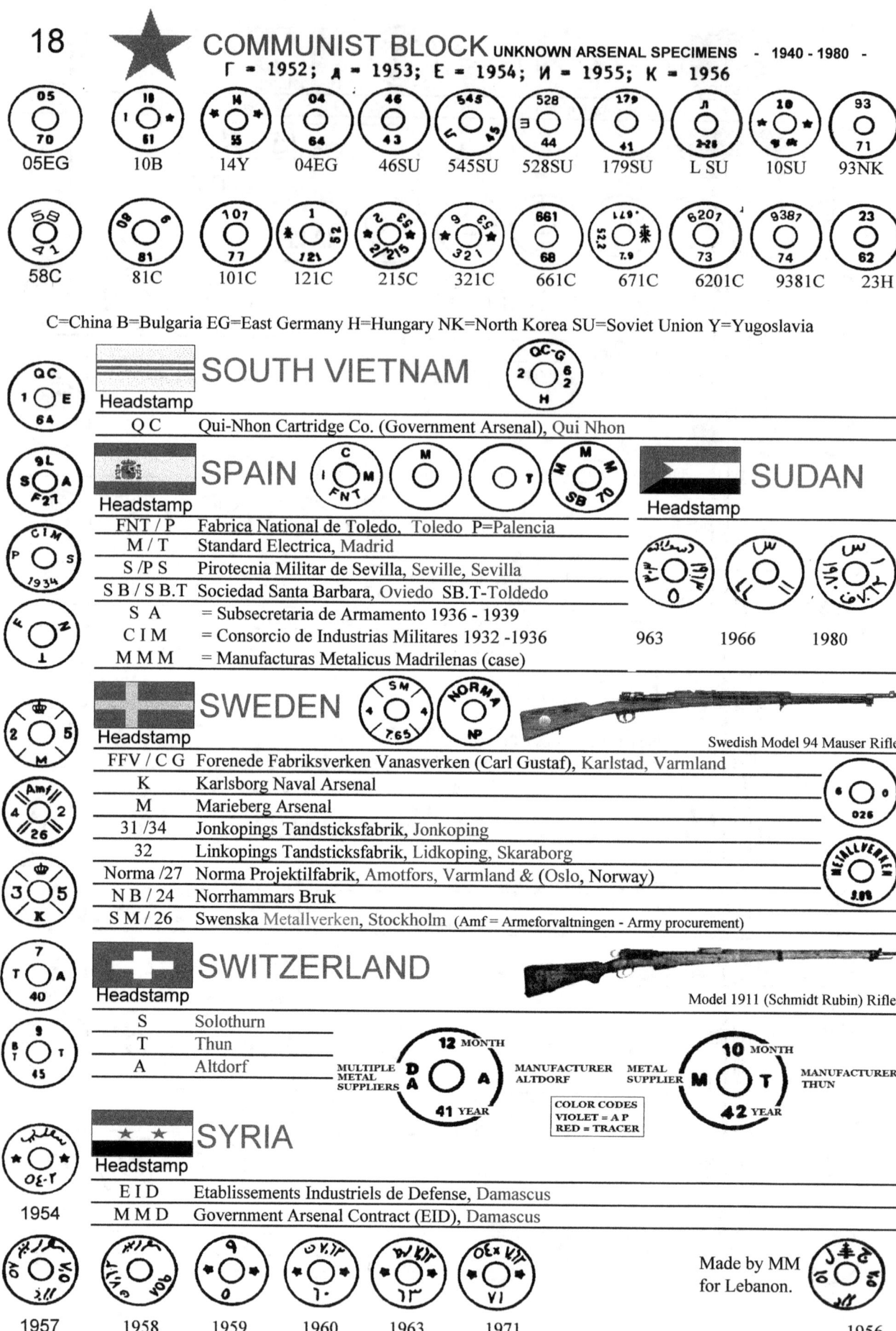

TAIWAN

Headstamp

60A	State Factory 60, Kao Hsiung

THAILAND

Headstamp

RTA	Royal Thai Army Arsenal, Bangkok
TA	Thai Arms, Bangkok

TURKEY

Headstamp

Turkish Model 93 Mauser Rifle

TC-FS	(Turkiye Cumhuriyeti - Turkish Republic) Fabrikalar Iskenderun, Iskenderun
TC-MKE	(Turkiye Cumhuriyeti - Turkish Republic) Makina ve Kimya Edustrisi, Kuruma
TC-AFA	(Turkiye Cumhuriyeti - Turkish Republic) Askeri Fabrikalar Mamulati

UNITED KINGDOM

Headstamp

#4 mk 1
#5 mk I Jungle Carbine

B / BC	Birmingham Metal and Munitions Co Ltd., Birmingham, Waltham Abbey, Essex
BD	Halls Telephone Company, Burgfield
BE	Royal Ordnance Factory, Swynerton, Blackpole, Worcester
BM	British Munitions Company, London
BLANCH	J. Blanch & Sons, London
BRMRC	British Manufacturing & Research Company, Grantham, Lincoln
CP	Crompton Parkinson Ltd., Guiseley, Yorkshire
C-P	Crompton Parkinson Ltd., Doncaster, Yorkshire
E / ELEY	Eley Brothers Limited, London
G /GB	Greenwood & Batley, Leeds
GBF	Greenwood & Batley, Farnham
G 18 F 1	Government Factory, #1, Blackheath
GA	Grenfell & Accles, Birmingham
GF 3	Government Factory, #3, Blackpole
H	Halls Telephone Company, Dowlais
HN	Royal Ordnance Factory, Hirwan, South Wales
ICI	Imperial Chemical Industries Limited, Birmingham
K 2	Kynoch, Imperial Chemical Industries Limited, Standish
K 4	Kynoch, Imperial Chemical Industries Limited, Yeading, Hayes, Middlesex
K 5	Kynoch, Imperial Chemical Industries Limited, Kidderminster, Worcestershire
KN	Kings Norton Metal Company Limited, Abby Wood, Kent, London
K/KYNOCH	Kynoch, Imperial Chemical Industries Limited, Birmingham
L	Lorenz Ammunition and Ordnance Company, Millwall, London
L	Ludlow and Company, Wolverhampton, Staffs
MAXIM	Maxim Arms Company, London
RC/RH	Raleigh Cycle Co., Ltd., Nottingham
RG	Ministry of Supply Factory, Radway Green
RL	Royal Laboratory, Woolwich, Kent, London
RTS	Richard Threlfall & Sons (explosive anti-zeppelin cartridges only)
RW	Rudge Whitworth Limited, Tyseley
SR	Royal Ordnance Factory, Aycliffe, Spennymoor
ST	Royal Ordnance Factory, Steeton

UNITED STATES

M-1 Garand Rifle

M-1 Carbine

Headstamp		
A A Co	American Ammunition Company, Oak Park, Illinois & Muscatine, Iowa	
A N	Twin Cities Ordnance Plant, Minneapolis, Minnesota	
A O	Allegany Ordnance Plant, Cumberland, Maryland	
B & M	Brass & Metall Manufacturing Co. Kansas City, Missouri (10.35mm Vetterli only)	
B N	St. Louis Ordnance Plant, St. Louis, Missouri	
C D L	C.D. Leet, Springfield, Massachusetts	
C N	Lake City Ordnance Plant, Independence, Missouri	
COLT	Colt Incorporated, Hartford, Connecticut	
D	E.I. Dupont de Nemours Company, Pompton, New Jersey	
D E N	Denver Ordnance Plant, Denver, Colorado	(Remington Arms Co.)
D M	Des Moines Ordnance Plant, Des Moines, Iowa	(U.S. Rubber Co.)
E C	Evansville - Chrysler Ornance Plant, Evansville, Indiana	
E C S	Evansville - Chrysler - Sunbeam Electric Ornance Plant, Evansville, Indiana	
E W	Eau Claire Ordnance Plant, Eau Claire, Wisconsin (U.S. Rubber Co.)	
F/FC	Federal Cartridge Company, Anoka, Minnesota	
F/F A/FAL	Frankford Arsenal, Philadelphia, Pennsylvania (SL* tools removed from St.Louis)	
FVV & Co.	Fitch Van Vechten & Company, New York, NY	
G E	General Electric Co., Cleveland, Ohio	
K B W	Kathodion Bronze Works, Nyack, NY	
K S	Allegheny Ordnance Plant, Cumberland, Maryland (Kelly Springfield Tire Co.)	
L C	Lake City Ordnance Plant, Independence, Missouri (Remington Arms Co.)	
L M / R L	Lowell Ordnance Plant, Lowell, Massachusetts (U.S. Ctg. Co.)	
M	Milwaukee Ordnance Plant, Milwaukee, Wisconsin	
M A X I M	Maxim Munitions Corporation, Waterton, New York	
N A Co	Newton Arms Company, Buffalo, New York	
N C	National Conduit & Cable Co. Hastings on the Hudson, New York/became NCI	
N C I	National Brass & Copper Tube Co. (National Conduit) Hastings on the Hudson, N.Y.	
P C	Kings Mills Ordnance Plant, Kings Mills, Ohio (Peters Cartridge Co.)	
P C Co	Peters Cartridge Company, Ohio	
PETERS	Peters Cartridge Company, Cincinnati, Ohio	
R A	Remmington Arms Company, Bridgeport, Connecticut	
R A H	Remmington Arms Company, Hoboken, New Jersey	
R A S	Remmington Arms Company, Swanton, Vermont Formerly RHA Co (1917)	
R/R H A Co	Robin Hood Ammunition Company, Swanton, Vermont	
REM-UMC	Remmington Arms - Union Metallic Cartridge Co., Bridgeport, Connecticut	
S A	Savage Arms Corporation, Chicopee Falls, Massachusetts	
S A Corp	Savage Arms Corporation, Chicopee Falls, Massachusetts	
S A W	Sage Ammunition Company, Middletown, Connecticut	
S C C	Standard Cartridge Company, Pasadena, California	
S L	St. Louis Ordnance Plant, St.Loius, Missouri	
S & W	Smith & Wesson Ammunition Company, Rock Creek, Ohio	
T C/T W	Twin Cities Ordnance Plant, Minneapolis, Minnesota (Federal Cartridge Co.)	
U M C	Union Metallic Cartridge Company, Bridgeport, Connecticut	
U/UT	Utah Ordnance Plant, Salt Lake City, Utah (Remington Arms Co.)	
U S	United States Cartridge Company, Lowell, Massachusetts	
W R A Co.	(WRA) (Winchester) Winchester Repeating Arms, New Haven, Connecticut	
W/W C C	Western Cartridge Company, East Alton, Illinois	
WESTERN	Western Cartridge Company, East Alton, Illinois	
WISE	Wise Manufacturing Company, Watertown, New York	

Browning Model 1922

Model 1898 Krag Carbine

Model 1911

Model 1917 U.S. Enfield Rifle

Model 1903 Springfield Rifle

UNITED STATES

Headstamp	Signal-Pirotechnic & Large Caliber Manufacturers until 1945	
B	Bridgeport Brass Co., Bridgeport, Connecticut	.50 Cal
DURA	Dura division of Detroit Harvester Corp., Toledo, Ohio	20mm Oerlikon
E K	Eastman Kodak, Rochester, New York	20mm Oerlikon
FAPS	Frankford Arsenal Pirotechnic Signal, Philadelphia, Pennsylvania	Signal
I F S	International Flare & Signal Co., Tippercanoe City, Ohio	Signal
L D F	Liberty Display Fireworks Co., Danville, Illinois	Signal
NOEN	Naval Ordnance Engineering Laboratory, Dalhlgren, Maryland	20mm Oerlikon
R F	Rockland Fireworks Co., Boston, Massachusetts	Signal
S D	Sparklet Devices Inc., Dover, Ohio	.50 Cal
S M Co	Stant Manufacturing Co., Connersville, Indiana	.50 Cal
T E I	Triumph Explosives Inc., Elkton, Maryland	Signal
V F M	Vitale Fireworks Manufacturing Co., New Castle Pennsylvania	Signal
U F	United Fireworks Co Manufacturing Co., Dayton, Ohio	Signal

EARLIER U.S. AMMUNITION COMPANIES

A.J.	Alton Jones, Portland, Oregan
A B & C Co.	American Buckle & Cartridge Company, West Haven, Connecticut
A	American Cartridge Company, Kansas City, Missouri
A. A. Co.	Atlantic Ammunition Company, New York, N.Y.
A C & Co.	Austin Cartridge Company, Cleveland, Ohio
	B.C. English, Springfield, Massachusetts
	Burnside Rifle Company, Providence, Rhode Island
	California Powder Works, Santa Cruz & San Francisco
	Central Cartridge Company, Kansas City, Missouri
C.C. Co.	Clinton Cartridge Company, Chicago, Illinois
C / C.C.C.	Creedmore Cartridge Company, Barberton, Ohio
C.T.M. Co.	Crittenden & Tribbals Mfg. Company, South Coventry, Connecticut
D.C.Co.	Delaware Cartridge Company, Wilmington, Delaware
	E. Remmington & Sons, Herkimer & Ilion, New York
	Elam O. Potter, New York, N.Y.
	Ethan Allen & Company, Worcester, Massachusetts
H.B.Fisher	H.B. Fisher, Philadelphia, Pennsylvania
	H.W. Mason & Company, South Coventry, Connecticut
	Hall & Hubbard, Springfield, Massachusetts
	Hazard Powder Company, Hazardville, Connecticut
	Hoffman Arms Company, Cleveland, Ohio
	Horstman Brothers & Allison, New York, N.Y.
	Hoxsie Ammunition Company, Chicago, Illinois
LIBERTY	Liberty Cartridge Company, Mt. Carmel & Sioux City, Connecticut
	Massachusetts Arms Company, Chicapee Falls, Massachusetts
M.F.A. Co.	Meridan Firearms Mfg. Company, Meriden, Connecticut
	Merrill Patent Firearms Company, Baltimore, Maryland
	National Projectile Works, Grand Rapids, Michigan
	New Haven Arms Company, New Haven, Connecticut
	New York Metallic Ammunition Company, New York, N.Y.
	Paultney & Trimble, Baltimore, Maryland
	Phoenic Cartridge Company, South Coventry, Connecticut
	Sharps Rifle Works, Hartford, Connecticut
So.C.Co.	Southern Cartridge Company, Houston, Texas S.C.Co. = Savannah, Georgia
Speer	Vernon D. Speer, Lewiston, Idaho
	Standard Cartridge Company, Pinales, California
	Volcanic Repeating Arms Company, New Haven, Connecticut
	Watervliet Arsenal, Watervliet, New York
	Worcester Cartridge Company, Worcester, Massachusetts
	Worcester Metallic Cartridge Company, Worcester, Massachusetts

U.S. Small Arms Inspectors Initials

AC	Alexander Cameron Colt 1940
ACD	A.C. Dieffenbach, Remington-Lee M1884 Rifles 1893-1894
ACP	A.C. Perrin, Colt 1935
ACT	A.C. Trego, Smith & Wesson .45 M1917 Revolvers 1918
AHF	Andrew H. Forsythe Colt M1911 .45 Pistol 1917
AJB	Aldeige J. Bessette Colt 1940
ALH	A.L. Hallstrom Colt M1911 .45 Pistols and Smith & Wesson Revolvers 1916-1917
ALW	A.L. Woodworth Colt .38 Revolvers 1905-1928
AWE	Arthur W. Evans, Remington-UMC M1911 .95 Pistol 1917-1918
B	Paul M. Busby, Remington-UMC M1911 .45 Pistol 1917
CAB	Charles A. Brand, Smth & Wesson M1889 .38 Revolvers, Lee-Winchester 6mm Rifles 1899-1900
CES	Clarence E. Simpson Colt 1939
CFD	Charles F. Dupee Colt 1937-1938
CFR	Charles F. Rogers Colt 1917
CFU	C.F. Ulrich Gunner, USN Colt and Smith & Wesson Revolvers 1905
CGH	Charles G. Howe, Colt 1917
CJV	C.J. Van Amburgh Colt Machine Guns 1912
CSR	Charles S. Reed, Colt 1938-1940
DAT	D.A. Turner Colt M1911 .45 Pistols 1914-1915
DMK	David M. King, Colt 1898-1905
DMT	Daniel M. Taylor, Colt .38 Revolvers 1892
E	Arthur W. Evans, Remington-UMC M1911 .95 Pistol 1917-1918
ECP	Edward C. Perry Colt 1937-1940
EEC	E.E. Chapman, Remington-UMC M1911 .45 Pistol 1918-1919
EFJ	E.F. Jarrard Holsters Rock Island 1902
EH	Edward Hooker, Remington M1867 Pistol 1867
EHD	Elbert H. Dewey Colt M1911 .45 Pistols M1903 .30 Rifles 1909-1917
ELF	Elbert L. Ford, Colt 1938-1941
ELW	E.L. Wunler, Colt 1903
ELW	Edson L. Wood Colt 1940
EMCF	Earl Mcfarland, M1 .30 Rifle 1942-1943
FB	Frank Baker, Colt M1909 .45 Revolvers 1909-1917
FBA	F.B. Austin, Colt M1911 .45 Auto Pistol 1917
FDH	Filser D. Horrert Colt 1940
FHT	Feno H. Traux, Hi-Standard .22 Pistols 1941-1942
FJA	Frank J. Atwood, M1911A1 .45 Auto Pistols Made By Ithaca, Union Switch & Signal
FJA	Frank J. Atwood, Remington, 30 M1903A3 Rifles, National Postal Meter .30 M1 Carbine 1942-1944
FK	Frank Krack, Rock Island Inspector, Colt M1911A1 .45 Pistols, M1903A3 Rifles 1940
GAW	George A. Woody, M1 .30 Rifle, Colt 1929-1932 and 1941-1944
GEG	George E. Goll Civilian 1940-1944 .45ACP M1928A1 Savage Sub-Machine Gun
GHS	Gilbert H. Stewart, S&W M1917 and Colt M1917 .45 Revolvers, Colt M1911 and M1911A1 .45 Pistols 1915-1919, 1938-1940, M1 .30 Rifle 1942
GPH	George F. Howland Colt 1939
GRG	G.R. Goring M1903 Rifles 1906-1910
GWW	George W. Wassner Colt 1939
HD	Smith & Wesson Victory Revolvers 1942-1945
HFL	Harry F. Lunch Colt 1939-1940
HJL	Harold J. Labonte Colt 1939
HO	Henbert O'Leary, Colt 1926-1929
HR	Harold Richards Colt 1940
HRB	Howard R. Booth Colt 1940
HS	Harrison Shaler Remington-Rand M1911A1 .45 Pistols 1945
HWK	Herbert W. Kerr Colt 1940
IJA	Issac Arnold Jr. M1892 .30 Krag Rifles, M1903 and M1905 .30 Rifles
JAB	John A. Bell, Colt M1895, M1902 and Smith & Wesson M1902 Revolver 1902-1903

U.S. Small Arms Inspectors Initials

JAB	John A. Brooks Jr. Colt 1940
JAH	John Howell M1882 Navy Signal Pistols
JBH	Joseph B, Hayes Colt 1940
JEH	Jay E. Hoffer Colt .38 Revolvers, Gatling Guns 1903
JFC	J.F. Coyle M1903 Rifles 1906-1907
JFH	John F. Harlan M1 .30 Rifle 1953
JHB	John H. Barrett .30 M1903 Rifles. ,45 ACP M1921 Sub-Machine Gun
JJC	John J. Callahan Colt 1940
JJL	John J. Lynch Colt 1940
JKC	John K. Christmas Singer M1911A1 .45 Pistol 1942
JLD	J.L. Doppman Jr. Colt 1936
JLG	James L. Guion, M1 .30 Rifles 1950-1953
JLH	James L. Hatcher, Colt 1938
JMG	J.M. Gilbert Colt Revolvers and M1911 .45 Pistols 1917-1918
JPM	J.P. Mc Guinness Smith & Wesson and Colt Revolvers 1905
JWM	James W. Mc Coy Colt .38 Revolvers 1927-1929, 1938
KM	Kenneth Morton, Colt 1905 .45 Pistol 1907-1908
LAS	Lawrence A. Stone, Colt 1940
LJP	Laurance Phelen Colt 1939-1940
MRM	M.R. Marsh Colt .38 Revolvers 1898
MS	Maurice Sherman Colt 1940
NFR	Norman F. Ramsey, M1 .30 Rifle 1944-1945
PJD	Peter J. Diffley, Colt 1941
PMB	Paul M. Busby, Remington-UMC M1911 .45 Pistol 1917
RCD	R.C. Downie, Union Switch & Signal M1911A1 .45 Pistols 1943
RLB	Remington M1903A3 Rifles 1942-1944
RS	Robert Sears, Colt M1911A1 .45 Pistols 1940-1945
RSJ	R.S. Johnson Colt 1940
RWC	R.W. Chandler Smith & Wesson, Colt Revolvers 1917
RZC	R.Z. Crane, Colt 1935
SGG	Samuel G. Green, Colt 1939
SHM	Stepnen H. Macgregor, M1 .30 Rifles and Carbines 1945-1947
SLG	Sidney L. Gibson, Hi-Standard .22 Pistols 1941
SPG	Samuel P. Green Col. USA M1903, M1 .30 Rifles 1938
SPS	Sidney P. Spaulding, Colt 1940
TLC	T.L. Childs Colt M1911 .45 Pistol 1917
TMH	Thomas M. Hervey, Colt 1938
TMJ	Thomas M. Jervy, Colt 1937-1938
TWH	T.W. Holmes, Colt 1926
TWH	Thomas W. Hafer Colt 1941
UN	Urban Niblo, Colt .38 Revolvers 1928
VAL	Viotto A. Luukkonen Colt 1940
WAB	William A. Borden, Colt 1936-1939
WB	Waldemar Broberg, Colt, Smith & Wesson Victory Revolvers, Colt M1911A1 .45 Auto Pistols 1941
WBW	William B. Whittelsky, Winchester-Lee 6mm Rifle
WEH	W.E. Hosmer Springfield M1903 .30 Rifles and Colt M1911 .45 Pistols 1905-1915
WEH	William E. House, Colt 1938
WES	W.E. Strong Colt M1911 ,45 Pistols, M1903 .30 Rifles 1909-1917
WG	W. Ganeard Colt .38 Revolvers 1901-1902
WGP	Walter G. Penfield, Colt M1911 .45 Pistols 1909-1914

U.S.S.R.

Headstamp Soviet Union

Mosin Nagant Model 91/30 Carbine

Headstamp	Factory
2	Royal Ordnance Factory, Woolwich, (England)
3	Soviet Plant, Ulyanovsk
7	Soviet Plant, Vympel, Khabarovsk Territory
11	Prvi Partisan, Titovo, Uzice, (Yugoslavia)
17	Barnaul Machine Tool Plant, Barnaul
21	Zaklady Metalowe (MESKO), Skarzysko-Kamienna (Poland)
23	Matravideki Femmuvek, Sirok (Hungary)
24	Norrhammars Bruk (brass cases only) (Sweden)
25	Vulcans Tandsticksfabrik, Tidaholm, (Sweden)
26 / 35	Swenska Metallverken, Vasteras, (Blikstorp 1954-65) (Sweden)
27	Norma Projectilfabrik, Amotfors, (Sweden)
29	Valtion Patruunatehdas, Lapua, (Finland)
32	Linkopings Tandsticksfabrik, Lidkoping, (Sweden)
33	Cesklovenska Zbrojovka Akciova Spolecnost v Brne, Brno, Bystrica (Czechoslovakia)
28 /34	Jonkopings Tandsticksfabrik, Jonkoping, (Sweden)
38	Soviet Government Arsenal, Yuryevets
54	Panstwowe Wytwornie Uzbrojenia, Fabryka Amunicji, Skarzysko-Kamienna (Poland)
60	Soviet Government Arsenal, Frunze, Kirghiz
88	Western Cartridge Company, East Alton, Illinois (United States)
122	Sloboda Cacak, Cacak (Yugoslavia)
188 / L V E	Novosibirsk Low Voltage Equipment Plant, Novosibirsk
270	Soviet State Arsenal, Lugansk, Ukraine
304	Soviet State Arsenal, Moscow
187/539 T	Tulskia (Tula) Patron (Cartridge) Zavody (Works), Tula
710 /711	Soviet State Arsenal, Podolsk

МЕТАК
МИТРАЉЕЗ
ОБИЧНИМ
ПИШТОЉ
СЕРИЈА
ТЕШКИМ
ЗРНОМ

YUGOSLAVIA

Headstamp

Headstamp	Factory
B K	Barutana Kamnik, Kamnik, Slovenia
B T(3) E	Voino Tekniki Zavod, Kragujevac
I K / N K	Igman Konjic, Konjic, Bosnia
K P A	Kragugevac serbje Voini, Serbia
K V	Krusik Valjevo, Valjevo, Serbia
M B L	Milan Blagojevic, Lucani, Serbia
M O L	Marko Oreskovic, Licki Osik, Croatia
M Z K	Miloje Zadic, Krusevac, Serbia
P G	Probjeda Gorazde, Gorazde, Bosnia
P P U / 11	(PP) Prvi Partisan, Titovo, Uzice, Serbia
S C / 122	Sloboda Cacak, Cacak
S M B	Suvenir, Makedonshi Brod, Macedonia
S P S	Slobodan Princip Seljo, Vitez, Bosnia
S R B	Slavko Rodic, Bugojno, Bosnia
T V	Tito Vogosca, Bosnia

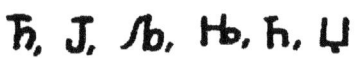

Ђ, Ј, Љ, Њ, Ћ, Џ

Cyrillic		English	
А	а	A	a
Б	б	B	b
В	в	V	v
Г	г	G	g
Д	д	D	d
Е	е	Ye, E	ye, e
Ж	ж	Zh	zh
З	з	Z	z
И	и	I	i
Й	й	Y	y
К	к	K	k
Л	л	L	l
М	м	M	m
Н	н	N	n
О	о	O	o
П	п	P	p
Р	р	R	r
С	с	S	s
Т	т	T	t
У	у	U	u
Ф	ф	F	f
Х	х	Kh	kh
Ц	ц	Ts	ts
Ч	ч	Ch	ch
Ш	ш	Sh	sh
Щ	щ	Shch	shch
Ъ	ъ	(")	(")
Ы	ы	Y	y
Ь	ь	(')	(')
Э	э	E	e
Ю	ю	Yu	yu
Я	я	Ya	ya

COLOR CODE SECTION
ARGENTINA

Caliber	Tip color	Function	Designation	Annulus Color
7.65x53.5	None	Ball	S	None
7.65x53.5	None	Ball, Heavy	SS	Green
7.65x53.5	Black	Explosive (HE)	R	Black / Tan
7.65x53.5	White	Incendiary	QI	White
7.65x53.5	Blue	Luminouis Tracer	TL	Blue
7.65x53.5	Yellow	SmokeTracer	TH	Yellow
7.65x53.5	Red	AP	P	Red
7.65x53.5	Maroon	High pressure test	ES	Green
7.65x53.5	Green	AP-T	LP	Green

CANADA & UNITED KINGDOM

Caliber	Tip color	Code	Other features	Code Translation	Annulus Color
.303	None	7 or 7Z		Light Ball	Purple
.303	Black	0.I		Observing	Black
.303	None	8Z		Heavy ball	Purple
.303	None	B4, B4Z	stepped bullet	Incendiary	Blue
.303	None	B6, B6Z		Incendiary	Blue
.303	Blue	B7, B7Z		Incendiary	Blue
7.92x57	None	BIZ, B2Z		Incendiary	Blue
.303	White	G4, G4Z, G6, G6Z		Tracer	Red
.303	Grey	G5, G5Z		Tracer	Red
.303	None	GI, G2, G3, G7, G8		Tracer	Red
7.92x57	None	GIZ, G2Z, G3Z		Tracer	Red
.303	None	HIZ, H2, H4, H7Z		Grenade launching	None
7.92x57	None	IZ, 2Z		Ball	Purple
.303	None	PGI, PGIZ	blue band on base	Practice tracer	Red
7.92x57	None	WIZ, W2Z		AP	Green
.303	None	WI, WIZ		AP	Green

Headstamp Letter Codes

Code	Function
B	Incendiary
D	Drill
E	Smoke Generator Discharger
F	Semi A P
FG	Semi A P Tracer
G	Tracer
H	Rifle Grenade
J	Illuminating
L	Blank
O	Observing
P	Practice
PG	Practice Tracer
Q	Proof
R	Explosive
U	Dummy
W	A P
WG	A P Tracer
NR	Non Rusting Powder
S	Smokeless Powder
SS	Semi Smokeless Powder
T	Black Powder
Z	Non Corrosive

Ammo box date codes

H = January	A = 1926
I = February	B = 1927
J = March	C = 1928
K = April	D = 1929
L = May	E = 1930
M = June	F = 1931
N = July	G = 1932
O = August	H = 1933
P = September	I = 1934
Q = October	J = 1935
R = November	K = 1936
S = December	L = 1937
	M = 1938
	N = 1939
	O = 1940
	P = 1941
	Q = 1942
	R = 1943
	S = 1944
	T = 1945
	U = 1946
	V = 1947
	W = 1948
	X = 1949
	Y = 1950
	Z = 1951

 ## FRENCH CARTRIDGE COLOR CODES & DESIGNATIONS UNTIL 1945

Cartidge	Description
7.5x54	Brass jacket, Black tip, black case mouth and black annulus = tracer "traceuse"
7.5x54	Black bullet, violet case mouth and violet annulus = heavy boattailed ball
7.5x54	Blue bullet tip, blue case mouth and annulus = incendiary (I) "incendiare"
7.5x54	Brass jacket = AP (P) "perforante"
7.5x54	Brass jacket, green tip, green case mouth and annulus = AP-T (TP) "traceuse perforante"
8x50R	Blackened bullet = armor piercing "perforante"
8x50R	Tin washed bullet = tracer "traceuse"
8x50R	Cupronickel "lead core" or solid bronze bullet = ball "balle"

 ## GERMAN CARTRIDGE COLOR CODES & DESIGNATIONS UNTIL 1945

Abbreviation	Description
Beschuss	Dark green coated base = proof load
B-Patrone	Chrome tip or black rear half of bullet and black primer annulus = observation (Beobactung Patrone)
Ex	Black or Red plastic case (rifle) / chrome case (pistol) = Exercise (Exerzier) (dry firing) no primer or powder
I.S. Ball	Green stripe across base = light ball - pointed bullet (leichtes spitzengeschoss) (practice) aluminum core
Nah-Patrone	Green case = light practice load (subsonic or low velocity)
P.m.K.	Black primer annulus = incendiary A.P. (Phospor mit Kern) early production have orange stripe across base
Platzpatrone	Red hollow wood or paper bullet - steel or brass case - 1 or 2 knurles on case = blank
S.m.E.	Blue primer annulus = heavy Ball (mild steel core) (spitzengeshoss mit eisenkern)
S.m.K.	Red or white primer annulus = A.P. "armor piercing" (spitzengeshoss mit kern) steel (Stahl) core
S.P.R.	Black Bullet (100%) & black primer annulus = incendiary
s.S. Ball	Green primer annulus = heavy ball - pointed bullet (schweres spitzengeschoss)
Ub.m. Zerl.	Black tip (3/4 of bullet) = self destroying (ubungsmunition mit zerlegung) w/ steel core (practice)
Werkzeug	Chromed (rifle) case & bullet (both hollow w/holes) = work tool for dismanteling machine guns

-Gehaertet (H)	tungsten carbide core bullet - "hardened core"
-Glspur	Glimmspur or "dim" tracer - add black tip (5mm wide)
-Lang (lg)	Longer projectile to match weight of ball loading for belt balance
-Lspur	Leutch spur or tracer - add black tip - (practice tracers have a green stripe across base)
-trop	Case mouth seal added that is the same color as primer annulus = tropic pack (tropen) (weather seal)
-v	verbessert = improved (velocity?)
Note: attributes designated with a dash as listed above may be combined with other type loadings.	
S.m.K. Lspur	Black tip & red primer annulus - A P Tracer
I.S. Lspur	Black tip - green stripe across base - Practice Tracer

METRIC CONVERSION CHART

Approximate Conversions to Metric Measures

Symbol	When You Know	Multiply by	To Find	Symbol
		LENGTH		
in	inches	2.5	centimeters	cm
ft	feet	30	centimeters	cm
yd	yards	0.9	meters	m
mi	miles	1.6	kilometers	km

Approximate Conversions from Metric Measures

Symbol	When You Know	Multiply by	To Find	Symbol
		LENGTH		
mm	millimeters	0.04	inches	in
cm	centimeters	0.4	inches	in
m	meters	3.3	feet	ft
m	meters	1.1	yards	yd
km	kilometers	0.6	miles	mi

 ## ITALIAN BREDA CARTRIDGE COLOR CODES UNTIL 1945

Cartridge	Description
8x59	Black bullet tip = observation (phosphorus) ignites on impact
8x59	Red bullet tip = armor piercing tracer
8x59	White bullet tip = armor piercing
8x59	Brass bullet (No color) = ball

IMPERIAL JAPANESE ARMY CARTRIDGE COLOR CODES UNTIL 1945

CASE MOUTH	6.5x50.5SR	7.7x58	7.7x58SR	7.92x57	12.7x81SR
PINK	BALL	BALL	BALL	BALL	xxxxxx
GREEN	TRACER	TRACER	TRACER	xxxxxx	TRACER
BLACK	xxxxxx	AP	AP	AP	AP-T
MAGENTA	xxxxxx	xxxxxx	Incendiary	Incendiary	xxxxxx
PURPLE	xxxxxx	xxxxxx	xxxxxx	xxxxxx	HEI
WHITE	xxxxxx	xxxxxx	HE (Petn)	xxxxxx	HEI (RDX)
RED	xxxxxx	xxxxxx	xxxxxx	xxxxxx	BALL
GREEN-WHITE	xxxxxx	xxxxxx	xxxxxx	xxxxxx	AP-T

IMPERIAL JAPANESE NAVY CARTRIDGE COLOR CODES UNTIL 1945

COLOR	7.7x56R Primer color	13.2x99 Annulus color	13x64B Projectile color
BLACK	BALL	BALL	BALL
WHITE	AP	AP	AP-T
RED	TRACER	TRACER	TRACER
GREEN	INCENDIARY	INCENDIARY	xxxxxx
PURPLE	HE (Petn) (blunt copper bullet)	xxxxxx	xxxxxx
YELLOW	xxxxxx	HEI (Petn)	xxxxxx
MAROON	xxxxxx	xxxxxx	(Rust color) HE (Petn)
RED-BROWN	xxxxxx	xxxxxx	(brown band) = HE-T (Petn)

Note 1: Blank & dummy cartridge headstamps are marked with 1 or 2 (dot) (example left)
Note 2: 13x64B all have either a live or dummy fuze in the projectile
Note 3: Cartridge sizes designated w/ R = Rimmed SR = Semi Rimmed
Note 4: Cartridge sizes listed as catagory without letter designation are rimless

SOVIET UNION CARTRIDGE COLOR CODES UNTIL 1945

Black bullet tip - red band = light armor piercing incendiary
Black Bullet tip = armor piercing
Green bullet tip - green primer annulus = tracer
Green case and bullet = silent partisan (subsonic)
Plain Bullet = standard ball
Purple bullet tip - red band = armor piercing incendiary tracer
Purple bullet tip = light armor piercing tracer
Red bullet-black tip-black primer annulus = heavy armor piercing incendiary
Red tip = explosive (tetryl) - incendiary
Silver (white) tip = light ball
Yellow bullet tip = heavy ball

UNITED STATES CARTRIDGE COLOR CODES & FEATURES UNTIL 1945

Black tip = armor piercing
Blackened case = tracer
Brass case - Rossett crimp = grenade blank
Brass case w/ vertical square canal from extracter groove = range dummy
Brass case w/ crimped case mouth and red wad = blank
Green on white field tip = frangible (bakelite - bonded lead powder compressed)
Light blue tip = incendiary
Longitudinal case corregations and or holes in case - no primer = dummy
No color or plain tip = ball
Orange tip = dark ignition tracer
Red tip = tracer
Silver tip (aluminum) = armor piercing incendiary
Stannic stained case (silvered) = high pressure test

Year	United States Armed Forces - Revolver Cartridge History
1800	.69 Simeon North Pistol
1861	.44 Remington Army Revolver
1861	.36 Whitney Navy Revolver
1865	.50 Army Inside Primed
1866	.50 Remington Revolver
1869	.45 Colt Martin Primed
1873	.45 Colt Inside Primed
1874	.45 Colt Revolver
1874	.45 Schofield Revolver (Calvary)
1874	.45 Remington Revolver
1911	.45 Colt Automatic Pistol
1917	.45 Colt Automatic Pistol Rimmed
1940	.38 Smith & Wesson Special - Navy

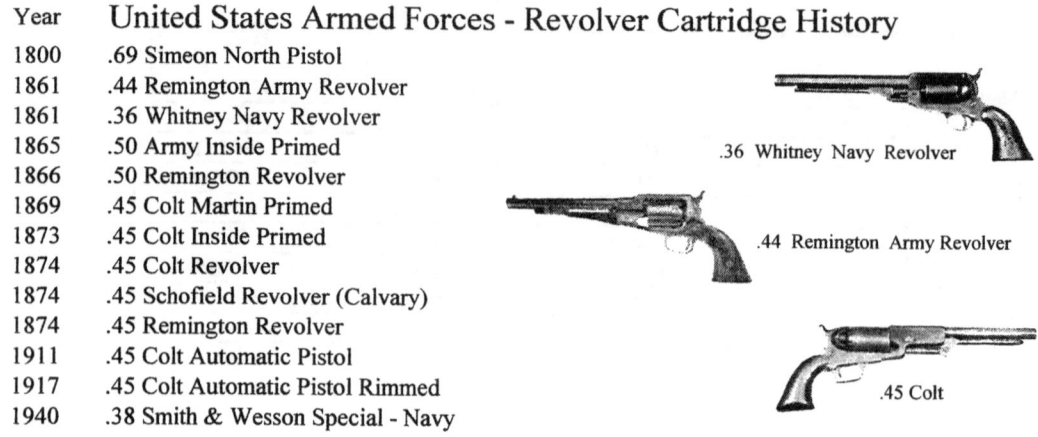

.36 Whitney Navy Revolver

.44 Remington Army Revolver

.45 Colt

United States   Civil War
1860   1865

Year	United States Armed Forces - Rifle Cartridge History
1850	.58 Springfield Minie Ball
1852	.52 Sharps Linnen
1860	.54 Burnside
1861	.58 Joslyn Carbine Rim Fire
1863	.50 Smith Carbine
1863	.50 Maynard
1865	.58 Miller Musket Rimfire
1868	.58 Allin Musket Inside Primed
1869	.58 Musket Centerfire
1870	.50-70 Springfield Rimfire
1870	.50-70 Springfield Inside Primed
1870	.50-70 Springfield Centerfire
1873	.45-70 Springfield Inside Primed
1873	.45-70 Springfield Centerfire
1892	.30-40 Krag
1897	.236 U.S. Navy
1903	.30-03 Springfield
1906	.30-06 Springfield
1918	.30 Pederson Device
1929	.276 Pederson Rifle
1941	.30 Carbine

Model 1855 Long Musket

Model 1859 Sharps Rifle .52 Linnen

1855 Harpers Ferry .58 Minie Ball w/ Maynard primer

.45-70 Springfield Rifle

.30-03 Springfield Rifle

Not all rifles in service were officially adapted.

*Joseph Rider of Newark, Ohio
Inventor
Remington Rolling Block Rifle*

YEAR	EVOLUTION OF THE CARTRIDGE - HISTORICAL TIME LINE
846 AD	A manuscript at the National Library in Paris describes a compound that measures (2) parts sulfur, (6) parts salt petre, (2) parts charcoal.
1313	The controversial date in which some believe Berthold Schartz, a German Franciscan Monk discovered gun powder.
1331	Used for propelling stone balls by the Moors.
1550	Probably the earliest form of cartridge was used by mounted troops who formed paper containers with a pre-measured amount of powder.
1774	Discovery of the detonating properties of fulminate of mercury.
1802	Duponts first began manufacturing of black powder in America.
1807	A Scottish Clergymen, Rev. Alexander Forsythe, working in the Tower of London obtained a patent for applying fulminate of mercury and other components to the ignition of gunpowder by means of a striking a blow.
1812	M. Pauli, Swiss born man working in Paris, developed a breech loading gun and complete self contained cartridge with removable head.
1814	Percussion caps invented by Joshua Shaw, an artist.
1825	Hall breach loader developed.
1827	First bolt action rifle developed by Von Dresye, (Needle gun)
1836	Pinfire cartridge invented by LeFaucheaux using cardboard and brass shot case.
1842	First percussion rifle used by the United States Armed Forces
1845	United States adapted percussion caps and Dr. Maynard invented his tape primer
1846	Houllier, a French gunsmith patented the first rimfire cartridge.
1848	Hunt cartridge developed lead ball-powder with hole in base of percussion cap.
1852	Mini ball used in Civil War and the invention of the linen Sharps cartridge.
1856	Smith & Wesson Volcanic cartridge developed.
1857	Smith & Wesson developed 1st metallic cartridge.
1859	J. White obtained his front loader patent.
1860	Burnside cartridge was patented by B. Foster
1865	1st metallic cartridge for armed services developed for the .58 Martin I.P.
1866	Large scale experiments with various new size caliber's, bullet compounds, case materials and ignition systems.

PISTOL, REVOLVER & RIFLE CARTRIDGES OF THE WORLD
COMPARATIVE MEASUREMENTS - CURRENT & HISTORIC

Cartridge Description	Bullet Diameter	Neck Diameter	Rim Diameter	Rim Type	Case Length	Overall Length
2.7mm Kolibri	.107	.139	.140	Rimmed	.37	.45
3mm Kolibri	.120	.151	.150	Rimmed	.32	.45
4.25mm Liliput	.167	.198	.198	Rimmed	.41	.56
5mm Clement Auto	.200	.222	.280	Rimless	.70	1.02
5mm Bergmann	.202	.230	.273	Rimless	.58	.95
5.45x18mm Soviet	.210	.220	.300	Rimless	.70	.98
22 Remington Jet	.223	.248	.440	Rimmed	1.27	1.56
5.5mm Velo Dog	.225	.248	.308	Rimmed	1.10	1.36
6mm Lee Navy	.244	.276	.448	Rimless	2.35	3.11
6.5x50.5 SR Japanese	.262	.290	.476	Semi-Rimmed	1.990	2.995
6.5 Dutch	.263	.297	.526	Rimmed	2.10	3.02
7mm "Baby" Nambu	.280	.295	.360	Rimless	.78	1.06
276 Pederson	.285	.315	.451	Rimless	2.00	2.86
7.35mm Carcano	.298	.325	.446	Rimless	2.12	2.880
7.65mm Roth-Sauer	.301	.333	.335	Rimless	.51	.84
7.5x54 French MAS	.304	.341	.486	Rimless	2.112	2.985
.30 Carbine	.305	.330	.356	Rimless	1.280	1.68
.30-40 Krag (30 Army)	.306	.332	.537	Rimmed	2.305	3.186
7.5x55 Schmidt-Rubin	.306	.335	.496	Rimless	2.145	3.51
7.62mm Tokerev	.307	.330	.390	Rimless	.99	1.34
7.65 Mannlicher	.308	.330	.334	Rimless	.85	1.10
7.65mm Luger	.308	.320	.391	Rimless	.75	1.15
7.63 Mauser	.308	.330	.390	Rimless	.98	1.36
.30-06 M2	.308	.338	.468	Rimless	2.481	3.34
.303 British	.308	.335	.522	Rimmed	2.205	3.31
35 S&W Auto	.309	.344	.248	Rimless	.68	.98
32 Automatic	.309	.336	.354	Semi-Rimmed	.68	1.02
7.62x54R Russian	.310	.332	.566	Rimmed	2.110	3.12
7.7x58 SR Japanese	.310	.336	.496	Semi-Rimmed	2.270	3.143
32 S&W	.312	.334	.374	Rimmed	.60	.93
32 Colt (Short)	.312	.314	.374	Rimmed	.62	1.00
32 Colt (Long)	.312	.314	.318	Rimmed	.90	1.25
7.5x55 Swiss	.317	.335	.407	Rimmed	.89	1.28
7.9x33 Kurz Patrone	.319	.352	.466	Rimless	1.30	1.88
8mm Rast-Gasser	.320	.332	.376	Rimmed	1.036	1.390
8mm Nambu	.320	.340	.413	Semi-Rimmed	.86	1.24
7.92x57 Mauser	.322	.351	.462	Rimless	2.238	3.160
8mm Lebel Revolver	.323	.350	.400	Rimmed	1.06	1.45
8mm Danish Krag	.323	.355	.575	Rimmed	2.26	3.20
8x51 Lebel	.324	.350	.324	Rimmed	1.978	2.953
8mm Murata	.329	.361	.558	Rimmed	2.05	2.90
9mm Browning	.355	.376	.400	Rimless	.80	1.10
9mm Glisenti	.355	.380	.392	Rimless	.75	1.15
9mm Ultra	.355	.374	.366	Rimless	.72	1.02
9mm Steyr	.355	.380	.380	Rimless	.90	1.30
9mm Federal	.355	.382	.435	Rimmed	.755	1.160
9mm Luger	.355	.380	.394	Rimless	.754	1.15

PISTOL, REVOLVER & RIFLE CARTRIDGES OF THE WORLD

COMPARATIVE MEASUREMENTS - CURRENT & HISTORIC

Cartridge Description	Bullet Diameter	Neck Diameter	Rim Diameter		Case Length	Overall Length
9mm Mauser	.355	.376	.390	Rimless	.980	1.38
9x23 Winchester	.355	.380	.392	Rimless	.900	1.245
9mm Win Magnum	.355	.380	.394	Rimless	1.15	1.545
380 Automatic	.356	.372	.374	Rimless	.68	.98
38 Colt (Short)	.357	.357	.430	Rimless	.75	1.10
38 Colt (Long)	.357	.358	.432	Rimmed	1.02	1.32
38 Special	.357	.379	.440	Rimmed	1.16	1.55
357 S&W Magnum	.357	.379	.440	Rimmed	1.29	1.51
357 Magnum	.357	.375	.433	Rimmed	1.58	1.96
357 SIG	.357	.381	.424	Rimless	.865	1.140
38 Auto & Super Auto	.358	.380	.405	Rimless	.90	1.28
9.8mm Auto Colt	.378	.404	.405	Rimless	.912	1.268
38 S&W	.359	.386	.430	Rimmed	.78	1.20
9mm Makarov	.362	.384	.396	Rimless	.70	.96
9.5mm Turkish Mauser	.389	.411	.610	Rimmed	2.35	3.015
40 S&W Auto	.400	.423	.424	Rimless	.850	1.135
10mm Auto	.400	.422	.424	Rimless	.99	1.25
41 Colt (Short)	.400	.404	.430	Rimmed	.89	1.04
41 Colt (Long)	.400	.404	.430	Rimmed	1.12	1.38
41 Action Express	.410	.432	.394	Rebated	.865	1.16
41 Remington Mag	.410	.432	.486	Rimmed	.128	1.60
10.4mm Italian	.422	.444	.505	Rimmed	.89	1.25
44 Merwin & Hulbert	.424	.442	.502	Rimmed	1.15	1.54
44 S&W Russian	.430	.457	.515	Rimmed	.96	1.43
44 S&W Special	.430	.457	.514	Rimmed	1.15	1.60
44 Auto Magnum	.430	.457	.472	Rimless	1.30	1.620
11mm Murata	.432	.465	.632	Rimmed	2.35	3.12
44 Webley	.436	.470	.502	Rimmed	.69	1.10
44 Bull Dog	.440	.470	.502	Rimmed	.58	.96
44 Colt	.443	.450	.482	Rimmed	1.10	1.50
11.75mm Montenegrin	.445	.472	.555	Rimmed	1.40	1.73
11mm French service	.451	.449	.490	Rimmed	.71	1.20
11mm German service	.451	.449	.509	Rimmed	.96	1.20
45 Winchester Mag	.451	.475	.482	Rimless	1.195	1.55
45 Webley	.452	.471	.504	Rimmed	.82	1.15
45 Auto Short	.452	.476	.476	Rimless	.860	1.16
45 Automatic	.438	.442	.468	Rimless	.891	1.275
455 Webley MkII Rev	.454	.476	.534	Rimmed	.78	1.22
45 Government Colt	.454	.478	.505	Rimmed	1.10	1.45
45 S&W Schofield	.442	.476	.518	Rimmed	1.108	1.422
45 Colt	.454	.476	.512	Rimmed	1.30	1.60
450 Revolver	.455	.475	.510	Rimmed	.69	1.10
455 Webley Auto	.455	.473	.500	Semi-Rimmed	.92	1.20
455 Colt	.455	.473	.530	Rimmed	.86	1.35
476 Enfield	.472	.474	.530	Rimmed	.86	1.34
50 Action Express	.500	.540	.514	Rebated	1.280	1.612
50 Remington Army	.508	.532	.665	Rimmed	.875	1.25

TRANSLATION SECTION
CHINA

穿	A P
釖 鉬 鋼 鋼	Brass
夾	Ammo in clips
毛 重	Gross Weight
燃 燃 烌	Incendiary
鉄 鈇 铁	Iron case
公斤	Kilograms
漆	Lacquered case
批	Lot
普 晋 詧 普	Ball
手 手	Pistol
发	No. Rounds
鋼 鋼 鋼 鋼	Steel
曳 曳 曳	Tracer

一	1
二	2
三	3
四	4
五	5
六	6
七	7
八	8
九	9
十	0

BURMA

(Burmese consonant chart with IPA transliterations: k [k], kh [kʰ], g [g], gh [g], ṅ [ŋ]; c [s], ch [sʰ], j [z], jh [z], ññ [ɲ]; ṭ [t], ṭh [tʰ], ḍ [d], ḍh [d], ṇ [n]; t [t], th [tʰ], d [d], dh [d], n [n]; p [p], ph [pʰ], b [b], bh [b], m [m]; y [j], r [r], l [l], w [w], s [θ]; h [h], l [l], ø [?], ñ [ɲ])

CZECHOSLOVAKIA

Abbr.	Czechoslovak	English
cv	cvicny	Blank
cv-okraj	cvicny okrajovy	Blank rimmed
fe	ocel	Steel
kr	karabina	Carbine
nab	naboj	Cartridges
ostr	ostry	Ball
pi	pistolovy	Pistol
pz	prubojny zapalny	API
rd	redukovany	Practice
sk	skolni	Dummy
s / sv	svitief	Tracer
tz	tezkou ostry	Heavy ball
tz sv	tezkou svitici	Heavy tracer
z	zapalny	Incendiary

DENMARK

Abbr.	Dutch	English
br	brand-	Incendiary
kar	karabijn	Carbine
ls	losse	Blank
lsp	lichtspoor	Tracer
ms	messing	Brass
pbr	pantserbrand	API
ptn	patroon	Cartridge
pts	pantser-	AP
rb	rookswak buskruit	Smokeless propellant
sch	scherpe	Ball cartridge
zb	zwart buskruit	Black powder

FINLAND

Abbr.	Finish	English
	laatiko	Box
	hylsy	Cartridge case
	luoti, luodin	Bullet
	lentojuokot	For aircraft
	nalli	Primer
	panos	Charge weight
ps	panssari	AP
p.patr	patruuna	Cartridge
pist	pistooli	Pistol
	ruutipano	Propellant
syt	sytytin	Incendiary
vj	valojuova	Tracer

FRANCE

Abbr.	French	English
aa	arme automatique	Machinegun
	blanc	Blank
	acier	Steel
arm	amorces	Primer
cart.	cartouche	Cartridge
ch.	charge	Propellant weight
c	courte	Short
et.	etuis	Cartridge case
f / fl	fusil	Rifle
fm	fusil-mitrailleuse	Light-machinegun
fr	fusil a repetition	Bolt action rifle
l	longue	Long
	lourde	Heavy
	laiton	Brass
m / mle	modele	Model
mit	mitrailleur / mitrailleuse	Machine gun
o	ordinaire	Ball bullet
pm	pistolet mitrailleur	Submachinegun
	portee reduite	Short range
r	reglage	Spotting
rt	reglage tracante	Spotter tracer
t	tracante traceur traceuse	Tracer, Tracing
tired.	tir reduite	Gallery practice
tp	tracante perforante	AP-T
v.b.	viven-bessieres	Rifle grenade (cup type launcher)

HUNGARY

Abbr.	Hungarian	English
	nyomjelzo lovedek	Tracer
pct	panceltoro	AP
	pisztoly	Pistol
pu	puska	Rifle
	puskagranat	Rifle Grenade
	suly	Weight
	tolteny	Cartridge
	urmeret	Caliber
	vaktolteny	Blank Cartridge
	karabely	Carbine
	gyalogsagitolteny	Ball Cartridge

ITALY

Abbr.	Italian	English
	"Cartucce a pallottola"	Ball
	"Cartucce a mitraglia"	Multiball
	"Cartucce frangibile"	Frangible
	"Cartucce di esercitazion"	Exercise
	"Pallottola perferante"	AP
	"Cartucce per tire ridette"	Reduced range
	"Cartucce di salve"	Blank

NORWAY

Abbr.	Norwegian	English
	brann	Incendiary
	krutt	Propellant
	kule	Bullet
	les patron	Blank cartridge
	panserprosjektil	AP bullet
	panserprosjektil-brann	AP Incendiary
	skarpe	Ball
	sporlys	Tracer
	tennhette	Primer

POLAND

Abbr.	Polish	English
	ciezki	Heavy bullet
	cwiczebne	Training
	mosiezny	Brass
	naboj	Cartridge
	naboj slepy	Blank Cartridge
	pancero	AP
	pociskow	Bullet
	prochu	Propellant
	rok	Year
	smugowy	Tracer
	stalowa	Steel
	zapalajacy	Incendiary
	zwyklym	Ball

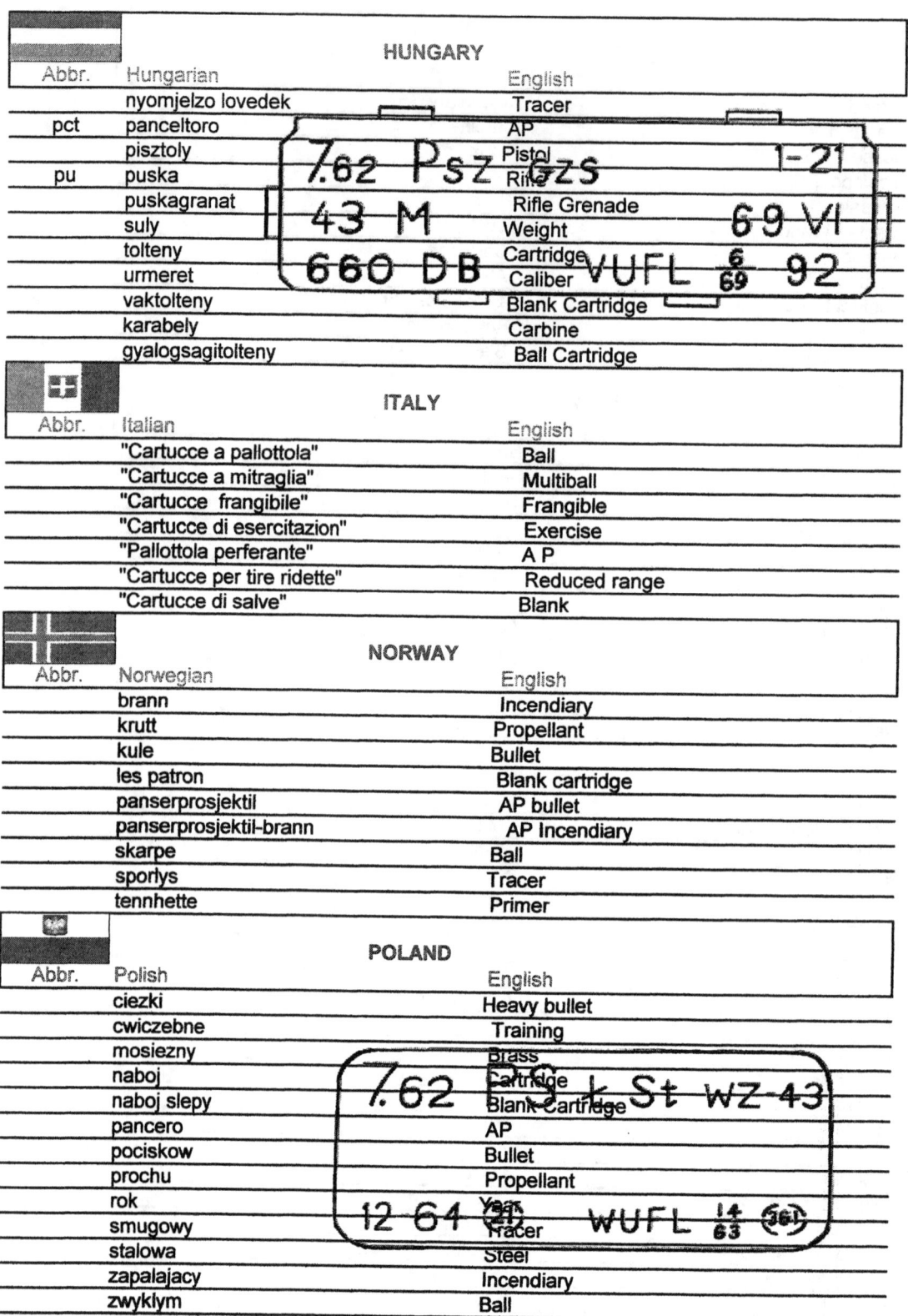

SOVIET UNION

Cyrillic	English	Code Translation
Б	B	AP
Б-30	B-30	AP 1930 pattern bullet
Б-32	B-32	AP 1932 pattern bullet
БС	BS	AP tungston carbide core
БС-40	BS-40	AP 1940 pattern bullet
БС-41	BS-41	AP 1941 pattern bullet
БСТ	BST	APT tungston carbide core w/ tracer
БЗТ-44	BZT-44	API 1944 pattern bullet incendiary
Д	D	Heavy ball bullet w/ lead core
ГЛ	GL	Brass cartridge
ГС	GS	Laquered steel cartridge
Х	Kh	Blank cartridge
ЛПС	LPS	Light ball w/ mild steel core
МДЗ	MDZ	HEI high explosive incendiary cartridge
ПСТ	PS or PST	Ball bullet with mild steel core
ПТ	PT	Tracer
ПЗ З	PZ or Z	Incendiary
Т-45	T-45	Tracer w/ 1945 pattern bullet

SPAIN

Abbr.	Spanish	English
	bala	Bullet
	capsula	Primer
	cartucho	Cartridge
	cartucho de guerra	Ball cartridge
	cartucho de instruccion	Dummy cartridge
	ejercicio	Practice
es	especial sobrecargada	High pressure test cartridge
	salvas	Blank
i	incendiaria	Incendiary
lp	luminosa perforante	APT
n	normal	Ball cartridge
p	perforante	AP
	polvora	Propellant
tl	trazante luminosa	Luminous tracer

SWEDEN

Abbr.	Swedish	English
brand	brand	Incendiary
k	karbin	Carbine
ml, M	modell	Model
nc	nitrocellulosa	Nitrocellulose
nband	normalband	Belted ball cartridge
ovnprj	ovnprojektil	Gallery practice bullet
P	pansar	AP
pptr	pansarpatron	AP cartridge
pprj	pansarprojectil	AP bullet
ptr	patron	Cartridge
ptrh	patronhylsa	Cartridge case
prj	projektil	Bullet
red lng	reducerad laddning	Reduced loading
sk	skarpa	Live cartridge
sl, slj	sparljus	Tracer
svkr	svartkrut	Black Powder

G. ROTH

Metallwerk, Metallwaren-, Patronenhulsen-, Zundhutchen-, Bleigschosse- u., Munition-Fabriken

CARTRIDGE HEADSTAMP IDENTIFICATION CODES

Size	Case No.	Cartridge Description
9.2x26R	7	Austrian Infantry Revolver
9.8x36R	44	Mauser "A" Base
11.2x36R	45	Austrian Model 67
11.2x41.5R	46	Mauser "A" Base
11.2x41.5R	47	Mauser "A" Base
9.8x45R	48	Mauser "A" Base
11.2x45.5R	49	Mauser "A" Base
11.2x51R	50	Kropatschek-Heissig
10.5x46.5R	51	Mauser "A" Base
11.2x45.5R	52	Mauser "A" Base
10.5x40R	53	Mauser "A" Base-Straight
11.2x60R	56	German Mauser
11x57.5R	61	Russian Berdan
11.15x58R	62	Austrian Werndl
10.2x61R	65	Swedish Jarmann
11.6x60R	66	Roumanian
11.15x60R	69	France and Greece Gras
11.15x36R	70	Austrian Model 82
10x51R	71	Mauser "A" Base
9.6x47R	74	Stahl
11.15x57.8R	76	Spanish
11.6x82.5R	77	English .450 3 1/4
11.5x18R	78	.450 Revolver
9.8x46.5R	84	Mauser "A" Base
10.5x42R	85	Mauser "A" Base
9x46.5R	88	Mauser "A" Base
10.1x47R	89	Mauser "A" Base
10.5x46.5R	90	Mauser "A" Base
9.8x41R	91	Mauser "A" Base
11x45.5R	92	Mauser "A" Base
10.1x51R	93	Mauser "A" Base
8x16.5R	97	.320 Revolver
8.5x17R	98	.340 Revolver
9.17.5R	99	Revolver
9.5x18R	100	.380 Revolver
8x19.5R	101	.320 Long Revolver
8.5x21.5R	102	.340 Long Revolver
9.5x23R	103	Revolver
9.5x24.5R	104	.380 Long Revolver
8.2x37.5R	107	Mauser "A" Base
10.5x46.5R	123	Mauser "A" Base
10.5x40R	126	Mauser "A" Base-Necked
11.6x60R	127	English .450 2.3"
13x38R	128	Mauser "A" Straight
11.2x29.5R	131	Gasser Revolver M 82
12.7x65R	134	English .500 2.6"
12.7x76R	139	English .500 3"
10.54x42R	142	Mauser "A" Base
10x60R	143	English .400 2.4"
11.6x65R	155	English .450 2.6"
9.1x50R	156	Straight
14.5x48.7R	157	Hochwild
12.7x43R	158	Maiser "A" Straight
9.8x40R	160	Mauser "A" Base
9.5x42R	161	Schieben
9.7x34.5R	162	Mauser "A" Base

G. ROTH — G. ROTH — G. ROTH

Metallwerk, Metallwaren-, Patronenhulsen-, Zundhutchen-, Bleigeschosse- u., Munition-Fabriken

CARTRIDGE HEADSTAMP IDENTIFICATION CODES

Size	Case No.	Cartridge Description
9.8x35R	163	Mauser "A" Base
9x38R	165	Mauser "A" Base
7.8x28R	166	Tesching
13x58R	176	Mauser "A" Straight
14.2x33R	177	Straight
6.8x28R	179	Tesching
11.3x51R	180	Mauser "A" Straight
11.5x19R	186	.455 Revolver Mk II Thin Rim
10.8x32R	191	44-40
9.2x51R	192	Mauser "A" Base
8.3x51R	193	Mauser "A" Base
9x53R	194	Mauser "A" Base
10.3x62.4R	200	Serbian
11.5x58.5R	202	Turkish
8.2x59.5R	203	Mauser "A" Base
11.3x48R	211	Mauser "A" Base
9.8x60R	216	Turkish
8x46.5R	233	Mauser "A" Base
12.7x60R	240	English .500 2.3"
11.5x58.5R	259	English .577/450
10.3x53.5R	274	.40-60 W.C.F
9x42R	276	Mauser "A" Base
11.5x58.5R	279	Necked
11.2x36R	287	Montenegrin Revolver
11.54x19R	288	.455 Revolver Mk II Thick Rim
8.2x57	289	Belgian
11.6x53R	293	.45-85 Colt
8x37R	296	Scheiben (Straight)
8x17.5	298	Auto Pistol
8.1x27R	304	Gasser Revolver
8.2x27.5R	304	Also refers to Revolver Model 98
8x42R	341	Mauser "A" Base
8x22.5R	350	Revolver
10.7x24.6R	352	Revolver
7.8x16.5R	353	Revolver
8x57	362	German Model 88
7x37R	387	Scheiben
7x30R	388	Scheiben
6.7x53.5R	393	Dutch Mannlicher
5.6x20R	400	.297/.230 Revolver
7.8x53.5	412	7.65 Turkish
5.2x34R	425	Kronprinz
8x41R	426	Revolver
6.8x19.6R	430	Revolver
8.2x50.5R	460	Austrian M 93
8.5x46.5R	464	Mauser "A" Base
9.3x47R	465	Mauser "A" Base
6.7x53.5R	474	Roumanian & Portuguese
12x39R	475	Mauser "A" Base Straight
8x35.8R	479	Mauser "A" Base
8.2x57R	481	Tapered
9.7x50R	494	Necked
6.7x54.8	502	Norwegian
6.3x21	518	Auto Pistol
6.25x37R	519	Tesching
9.5x47.8R	528	Scheiben
11.8x49.4R	543	Straight

G. ROTH G. ROTH G. ROTH G. ROTH

Metallwerk, Metallwaren-,Patronenhulsen-, Zundhutchen-, Bleigeschosse- u., Munition-Fabriken

CARTRIDGE HEADSTAMP IDENTIFICATION CODES

Size	Case No.	Cartridge Description
8.2x46.5R	553	8.15x46R Normal
9.2x57R	561	.360 2 1/4
7.9x45.5R	568	Schieben
6.5x25.8R	573	6.5x25.8R Tesching
7.2x56.7	574	Spanish
12.3x50R	578	Mauser "A" Base Straight
8.2x20.7R	592	Auto Pistol
8.2x50.5R	594	Jagd
11.2x36R	600	Hungarian Carbine
8x22.3R	609	Revolver
8.2x45	618	Jagd
7.8x17.5	619	.32 A.C.P.
7.3x19.5R	620	Revolver
11.4x51.8R	625	Mauser "A" Base
8x57R	626	Tapered-Necked
8.2x52R	629	Necked
9.6x59.8R	631	Necked
6.7x53.5	632	Mannlicher-Schoenauer
6.7x53.5R	633	Tesching
9.5x60R	634	Straight
9.2x72R	635	.360-2.8"
9x61R	636	Straight
6.7x57	637	Mauser
8.2x62R	638	Tapered-Necked
6.8x33R	639	Tesching
6.8x37R	640	Mauser "A" Base
6.8x42R	641	Tesching
9x66.8R	642	Straight
8x57R	643	Tapered
5.8x30R	646	5.5 Velo Dog
10.2x59.8R	648	Necked
7.2x56.7	649	Serbian
6.7x21.5	658	6.5 Bergmann # 3
8x57R	661	8x57 / .360
8.3x27.5R	662	Lebel Revolver M 1892
7.2x56.6	664	Mauser
9x69.5R	666	Necked
9.5x50.5R	667	Necked
8.2x72R	669	8x72/ .360
6.65x13.5	674	Auto Pistol
8.2x55R	679	Necked
8x50.7	681	Jagd
9x29.5R	682	Revolver
7.9x52.9R	683	Russian Moisen
8x38R	684	Russian Nagant Revolver
8.2x54.8R	696	Jagd
8.6x50.5R	691	Necked
5.8x36.4R	692	Tesching
8.2x18.8	696	Roth-Styer Model 7
9x56.2	700	Mannlicher-Schoenauer
8.2x52	701	Jagd
7.8x12.8	703	Roth-Sauer Auto Pistol
7.8x35.8R	704	Mauser "A" Base
7.5x46.7R	705	Jagd
11.15x61.8	707	Straight
9.2x82R	709	.360 -3 1/4
5.7x36.9	712	Tesching

G. ROTH

Metallwerk, Metallwaren-, Patronenhulsen-, Zundhutchen-, Bleigeschosse- u., Munition-Fabriken

CARTRIDGE HEADSTAMP IDENTIFICATION CODES

Size	Case No.	Cartridge Description
9x46.5R	715	Jagd
7.8x21	716	Mannlicher-Pistol M 1900
10.75x56.7R	717	Mauser & Mannlicher
9x63R	720	Necked
10.75x61	721	Jagd
10.75x59.8R	723	Necked
9.4x60	724	Jagd
11.15x61.9R	725	Straight
11.5x59.8	728	Schuler
5.2x17	730	Clement Auto Pistol
6.5x40R	741	Tesching
6.5x48R	742	Tesching
6.6x27.2R	746	Tesching
9.3x63.8	748	Jagd
8.25x37.6R	749	Tesching
5.7x32.8	751	Pistol
12.6x20.5R	754	.500 Revolver
8x72R	755	Straight Tapered
6.35x15.8	757	.25 A.C.P.
6.5x57.7	758	Portuguese
10.7x60R	759	Straight
9x61.8R	760	Necked
10.3x18.6	762	Auto Pistol
9.5x72R	770	Tapered
6.5x43R	775	Tesching
11x71.5	780	Schuler
11.8x74R	782	Straight
9x71	783	Peterlongo
8.8x29.3	784	.35 Winchester Self Loading
8.8x35	785	.351 Winchester Self Loading
5x36.6R	786	Tesching
8.2x56.6	788	Mannlicher Schoenauer
8x71	790	Peterlongo
6.5x41.5R	794	Tesching
9x71R	795	Peterlongo
8.2x50.5R	797	Jagd
8.2x52.8R	802	Jagd
5.5x35.5R	803	Vierling
8.2x59.2R	804	Necked
9x53.4R	805	Necked
6.35x22.4	806	Auto Pistol
8.2x58.8R	807	Necked
6.8x56.3	808	Jagd
9.5x56.7	811	Mannlicher Schoenauer
8.2x55R	813	Jagd
11.2x36.3R	826	Fruhwirth Carbine
9mm	892	Steyr-Hahn Pistol M 1911

ADDITIONAL ENTRIES & NOTES

D W M
Deutsche Waffen und Munitionsfabriken

Size	Case No.	Cartridge Description
7.6mm	5	Mauser Revolver
9mm	6	Mauser Revolver
10.6mm	7	Mauser Revolver
9x36R	8	Small Bore
12mm	17	Norwevian Remington
10.4mm	19	Italian Vetterli
11.55x40R	21	Target
9.5x47R	23	Target
11.2x47R	24	Target
9x47R	25	Target
11.55x50R	26	Target
11.55x50R	26A	Target
10X52R	27	Target
11.4x50R	28	Werndl
10.5x47R	29	Target
10x47R	30	Target
10x47R	31A	Target-A Base
8.1x42R	33	Target
11.5x35.4R	34	Werder Carbine
9.15x60R	35	Target
10.5x40R	38	Swiss Vetterli
10.75x58R	39	Russian Berdan
11.43	40	Roumanian Martini Henry
11.15x60R	41	Unknown
11.2x60R	41A	Mauser M 71/84
10.5x36R	42	Small Bore
12x50R	53	Target
8x36R	54	Small Bore
11x37R	55	Military
11.25x32.9R	57	Target
11.2x44R	58	Target
10.35mm	59A	Swiss Vetterli
11.43mm	70	.450-3 1/4 Straight
11.43mm	71	.450-3 1/4 Straight
12.7mm	72	.500-3"
12.7mm	72A	.500-3.4"
9.3x43R	73	Hunting
11.43mm	75	.450 W R No. 1
10.45x60R	76	Hunting
10.4x82	76B	Hunting
9.35x57R	77	Hunting
9.35x72	77A	Hunting
9.35x80	77B	Hunting
9.35x82.4	77C	Hunting
9.3x72R	77D	Normal
9.35x57	77E	Hunting
9.35x70R	77F	Hunting
11.43mm	78	.45-75 W.C.F.
8x57R	88A	Mauser "A" Base
8x57R	88B	Mauser-Flat Base
8x57R	88C	Hunting
8x42R	88D	Hunting
8x50R	88E	Hunting
8.1x57R	88F	Hunting

D W M
Deutsche Waffen und Munitionsfabriken

Size	Case No.	Cartridge Description
8x57	88G	Hunting
8x51	88H	Mauser Short
8x50R	88H2	Unknown
9.15x40R	91	Small Bore
9x38R	92	Small Bore
8x38R	93	Small Bore
7x57R	93A	Mauser "A" Base
7x57R	93B	Mauser
7x57	93S	Mauser
7x38R	94	Small Bore
9x36R	95	Small Bore
11.43mm	96	.450 2 3/8"
12.7mm	97	.500 2 1/4
11.2x52R	99	Target
11x52R	100	Target
10.5x52R	101	Target
10x46R	104	Target
9.5x46R	105	Target
10x42R	108	Target
12.4x42R	110	Target
11.43mm	122	.450 British Gatling
11x58R	132	Werndl M/77
11.15mm	140	Dutch Beaumont
10.8x47R	146	Target
10.75x33R	149	.44-40 W.C.F.
10.3x65R	164	Banziger
11.43mm	167	Portuguese Martini Henry
10.15mm	173	Swedish Jarmann
9x36R	174	Small Bore
11.4x55R	177	Hunting
9.3x36R	178	Hunting
9.5x47	179	Target
11x42	180	Target
12.4x40R	184	Target
10.10mm	187	Serbian Mauser M 71/80
11x28R	188	Target
11.4x50R	190	Target
11.43mm	191	.450-2 1/2
11.15x18R	192	.450 Revolver
11.35mm	192B	.45 Schouboe Auto Pistol
9.5x17.5R	193	.380 Revolver
8.1x16R	194	.320 Revolver
12.7mm	196	.500-2"
9.85x47R	198	Target
10.9x46R	199	Target
10.6mm	200	German Ordnance Revolver M /1879
10.6mm	200A	German Ordnance Revolver Flat Based
10.6mm	200B	German Ordnance Revolver Shot Case
12.3x40R	201	Small Bore
8.15x15.80R	202	.32 S&W Revolver
9.5x20.3R	203	.38 S&W Revolver
10.40x23.40R	204	.44 S&W Revolver
10.9x45R	205	Small Bore
11.43mm	206	Danish Remington

DWM
Deutsche Waffen und Munitionsfabriken

Size	Case No.	Cartridge Description
12.7mm	207	.500 W R No. 2
9.65x57	212	Hunting
10.25x69	214	Hunting
9.55x36	215	Small Bore
9.25x24.5R	218	.380 Long-Revolver
9.25x26.3	218A	.380 Long-Revolver
8.1x20.5R	219	.320 Long-Revolver
8.1x20.5R	219A	.320 Long-Revolver-"A" Base
10.5x17R	221	.442 Revolver
11.7x22R	228	.455 Mk I Revolver
10.75x26.5R	229	.442 Long-Revolver
11.50x32.8R	231	.450 Long-Revolver
8.1x16R	233	.320 Revolver
10.3x65R	237A	Target
11.35x45R	240	Hunting
9.2x40R	241	Hunting
11.5x24.8R	242	.44 S&W Russian Revolver
8x30R	244	Small Bore
9.35x80	246	Hunting
8.1x36R	249	Small Bore
10.2x20R	251	Small Bore
10.2x20R	251A	Small Bore "A" Base
9.5x46R	258	Target
8.15x15.80R	260	.32 S&W Revolver
9.5x20.3R	261	.38 S&W Revolver
9.5x20.3R	261A	.38 S&W "A" Base
8.1x20R	262	.32 Colt Revolver
9x26.5R	263	.38 Long Colt
14.7mm	267	.577-2 3/4"
11.43mm	268	.450-3 1/4 Straight
14mm	270	Belgium Comblain M /71
11mm	271	.43 Egyptian
11mm	272C	Spanish Remington
12.7mm	273	.500 Revolver
14.7mm	274	.577 Pistol
9x24R	276	Small Bore
9.5x50	283	Hunting
10.2mm	284	Revolver
11x50R	291	Beaumont
9.4mm	296	Dutch Revolver
14.7mm	298	.577 Snider 2"
7.50x30.3R	300	Revolver
11.7mm	301	Monteigny Mitrailleuse
11.5	307	Hotchkiss M /74
11.7x73	309	Hunting
11.35x50R	310	Target
7.92x94.5	318	Unknown
8x60R	319	Kropatschek
11mm	320	Cattle Killer
11mm	321	Cattle Killer
10.2x32R	329	.44-40 C.L.M.R.
11.35x59R	332	Target
8.1mm	336	Lee Nagant M /92
9.75x54.9R	339	Target

D W M
Deutsche Waffen und Munitionsfabriken

Size	Case No.	Cartridge Description
9.75x54.9R	339A	Target "A" Base
8x57R	357	Unknown
8x50R	358	Austrian Mannlicher
8x50R	358C	Mannlicher M /95
10.15mm	362	Turkish Mauser
8x57	366	Mauser
8x57R	366B	Mauser M /88 "A" Base
8x57JR	366D1	Mauser "B" Base
8x57	366J	Mauser M /88
8x51	366L	Mauser-Short M /88
8x51R	366L2	Unknown
8x57J	366N9	Drill Cartridge
7.65x54	367	Argentine Mauser
7.65x54	367A	Turkish Mauser
7.65x54	367C	Belgian Mauser
7.65x54	367E	Argentine Mauser
7.65x53	367L	Unknown
6.6x57	375	Hunting
7.62x54R	378	Moisen Nagant
7.62x58.5R	379	.30-40 Krag
7.62x63	379E	.30-06
7x57	380D	Spanish Mauser
7x57R	380H	Mauser "A" Base
7x57R	380J	Mauser
7x57	380L	Mauser
7x57	380M	Mauser
5.43x26.8	383	Revolver
8.15x58R	385	Danish Krag
8x56	388	Schmidt-Rubin
8x56	388D	Schmidt-Rubin
6.68x54	392B	Hunting
9.4x56R	393	Hunting
6.5x53	394	Dutch Mannlicher
6.5x53R	395C	Dutch Mannlicher
6.5x53R	395D	Roumanian Mannlicher
10.8x57R	397	Target
7.63mm	403	Mauser Automatic Pistol
7.63mm	403I	Mauser Automatic Pistol Drill Cartridge
6.5x57	404A	Model 88
10.5mm	409	Cattle Killer
10.5mm	409A	Cattle Killer
11.6mm	411	German Revolver
6.5mm	413A	Bergmann #3 Automatic Pistol
11.2x60R	414	Mauser M /71
5mm	416A	Bergmann #2 Automatic Pistol
5.2mm	416B	Pickert Revolver
7.4x57	419	Hunting
7.5mm	421	Swiss Ordnance Revolver
6mm	425A	U.S. Lee Navy Rifle
6.5x55	431C	Mauser
6.5x55	431F	Mauser Fatkoff
6.5x61	431L	Unknown
6.5x61R	431M	Unknown
5.6x61R	431M	Vom Hofe

D W M

Deutsche Waffen und Munitionsfabriken

Size	Case No.	Cartridge Description
5.6x61	431P	Vom Hofe
8x60R	439A	Portuguese Guedes
8x57R	446	.360
11.1x49R	447	Target
8mm	451	Bergmann #4 Automatic Pistol
7.5mm	451A	Bergmann No. 4A
9.05x17.8R	452	Revolver
7.7x56R	453	.303 Lee Medford
8.15x46R	455	Unknown
9mm	456	Bergmann Bayard Automatic Pistol
9mm	456A	Bergmann Bayard Automatic Pistol
9mm	456B	Bergmann Bayard Automatic Pistol
6.5x58	457	Portuguese Mauser
6.5x54	457A	Unknown
8mm	460	Bergmann #7 Automatic Pistol
7.5mm	460A	Bergmann #7A Automatic Pistol
7.8mm	461	Bergmann #5 Automatic Pistol
8x58R	462	Sauer & Sauer
8x48R	462A	Sauer & Sauer
6.5x58R	463	Sauer
6.5x48R	463A	Unknown
7.63mm	466	Mannlicher M1900 Pistol
5.7x33	467	Small Bore
5.7x33R	468	Small Bore
5x57R	469A	Target
7.65mm	471	Parabellum
7.65mm	471A	Parabellum Carbine
7.65mm	471I	Parabellum Drill Cartridge
8x50.5R	472	French Lebel M /93
6.5x72.5	473	Italian Carcano
9.5x73	473C	Miller & Greiss Magnum
9x70R	474B	Mauser .400/.360
9.3x62	474C	Mauser
9.3x62R	474D	Mauser
9.3x86	474F	Unknown
6.5x54	475A	Daudeteau
6.5x27P	476	Rimmed
6.5x53	477	Mannlicher Schoenauer
7.65mm	479	Browning .32 ACP
7.65mm	479A	Browning .32 ACP
7.65	479A1	Browning .32 ACP Drill Cartridge
9mm	480D	Parabellum Carbine
9mm	480C	Parabellum
9mm	480C3	Parabellum Drill Cartridge
6.5x51	481	Japanese Arisaka
7.5mm	482	Nagant-Norway & Sweden
5mm	484	Clement Automatic Pistol
9mm	487	Mauser Automatic Pistol - Export
9mm	487C	Mauser Parabellum M 12/14
8mm	488	Bergmann Simplex Automatic Pistol
6x58	489	Unknown
6.5x58R	489A	Unknown
6x58	489A	Unknown
11mm	490	Bergmann Automatic Pistol

D W M
Deutsche Waffen und Munitionsfabriken

Size	Case No.	Cartridge Description
9.2x57R	491	Hunting
9x57	491A	Mauser
9x57R	491B	Mauser
9x63mm	491D	Unknown
9x56	491E	Mannlicher Schoenauer
11.35mm	492	Bergmann Automatic Pistol
6.2x57	494	Hunting
10.75x70R	495	Magnum Mauser Rifle
7.65mm	497	Mannlicher Carbine M /96
6.35mm	508A	Browning .25 ACP
6.35mm	508A1	Browning .25 ACP
6.5x52	510A	Unknown
7x59.5	511C	Unknown
11.5x23.5R	513	.455 W & S Automatic Pistol
8x75R	514	Unknown
8x75	514A	Unknown
10.75x62	515	Unknown
10.75x68	515A	Unknown
6.5x52R	519	.25-35 WCF
6.5x52	519A	.25 Remington
10.75x62	523	Straight Case
8x56	528	Mannlicher Schoenauer
9.5x57	531	Mannlicher Schoenauer
11.75x88R	533	.450 No. 2 Express
5.6x52R	536	.22 High Power
5.6x35R	539	Vierling
9mm	540	Kurtz .380 Automatic Pistol
9mm	540I	Kurtz .380 Automatic Pistol Drill Cartridge
8x60mm	542	Unknown
8x60R	542A	Unknown
8x60R	542AM	Magnum
8x60R	542AMB	Magnum Bombe
8x60	542M	Magnum
8x60	542MB	Magnum Bombe
7.62x51R	543	.30-30
5.6x52R	545	.22 High Power
10.75x73	555	.404 Jeffrey
7x64	557	Brenneke
7x65R	557A	Brenneke
8x64	558	Brenneke
8x65R	558A	Brenneke
8x57	560	Mauser M /98
8x57JS	561	Mauser
9.3x70	569	.375 Holland
8x57	571	Drill Cartridge
7x63	572	Jurgen's Mauser
7x72R	573	Unknown
8x72R	574	Unknown
7x73	575	Vom Hofe
9mm	577	Styr Automatic Pistol
5.6x35R	578	.22 Hornet
11x31R	583	Mauser M /71/98

FA   FRANKFORD ARSENAL

- SPECIALIZED HEADSTAMPS -

H&R Reising

	Illuminating grenade 1917	Rifle grenade 1934	
	Rifle grenade 1918	Palma match 1934	
	Chemical warfare grenade 1920	National match 1937	
	National match 1921 (Tin Can)	.276 Cal Pedersen Berdan primer	
	Garand 1925	.30 Cal case primer test (T1) 1926	
	International match 1925	.30 Cal case primer test (T1E1) 1926	
	Pyrotechnical signal 1926	.30 Cal case primer test (T1E2) 1927	
	Chemical rifle grenade 1927	.30 Cal case primer test (T1E3)	
	Extruded process 1928	.30 Cal case non-chlorate primer test	
	Extruded process 1930	.30 Cal high presure test with .38 Cal primer	
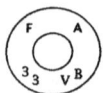	Viven Bessiere grenade 1933	International match 1927 -1929	
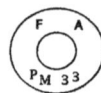	Palma match 1933	National match 1929	

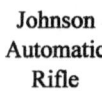
Johnson Automatic Rifle

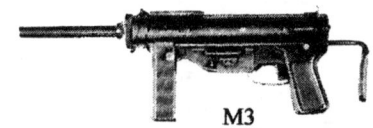
M3

46

UNITED STATES

Arsenal: Frankford
          Philadelphia, Pennsylvania

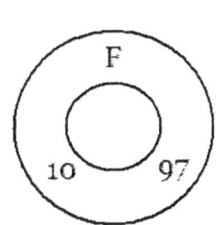

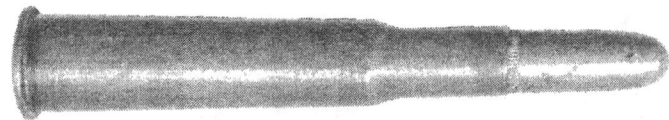

Headstamp   Side View

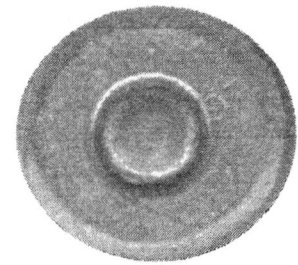

SPECIMEN DIMENSIONS

Rim Measurement: .537
Neck Measurement: .332
Bullet diameter: .306
Case Length: 2.305

Single Cannelure Bullet

OTHER DETAILS

Caliber: .30-40 Krag
Manufacture Date: 1897
Specialty: Ball
Cartridge type: Rifle

Overall Length: 3.186

General Information In 1886 the single cannelure bullet made its debut as the primary round for the .30-40 Krag rifle of the United States Military. It would soon be modified in an attempt to improve bullet pull and weather seal. Bullet length was 1.272 inches and the bullet weight was 220 grains.

UNITED STATES

Arsenal: Frankford
Philadelphia, Pennsylvania

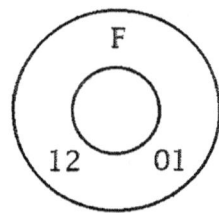

Headstamp

Side View

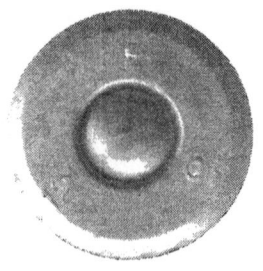

SPECIMEN DIMENSIONS

Rim Measurement: .538
Neck Measurement: .335
Bullet diameter: .308
Case Length: 2.308

3 Cannelure Bullet

OTHER DETAILS

Caliber: .30-40 Krag
Manufacture Date: 1901
Specialty: Ball
Cartridge type: Rifle

Overall Length: 3.96

General Information In 1900 this cupro-nickel jacketed bullet replaced the earlier (one cannelure) steel jacket to avoid rusting and excessive barrel wear. Two knurled cannelures were also added to the ball projectile (1.265) to produce this 3-cannelure bullet which provided a more secure water seal. However, complaints were then received that this modification gave the round a poor gas seal, so in 1902 a swedged base increased its diameter, which was referred to as the Lissak bullet. Both versions were lubricated with Japan wax and graphite.

UNITED STATES

Arsenal: Frankford
Philadelphia, Pennsylvania

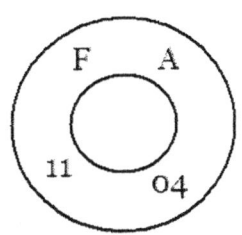

Headstamp   Side View

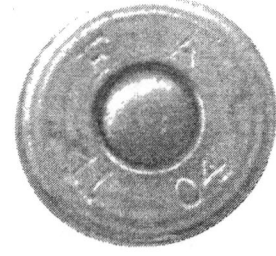

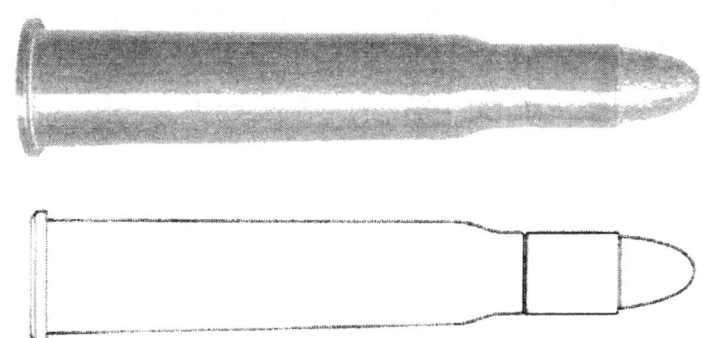

SPECIMEN DIMENSIONS

Rim Measurement: .541
Neck Measurement: .335
Bullet Diameter: .290
Case Length: 2.305

Sub Caliber Artillery Drill Cartridge

OTHER DETAILS

Caliber: .30 1903 Type
Manufacture Date: 1904
Specialty: Sub Caliber Ball
Cartridge Type: Rifle

Overall Length: 2.622

General Information: Actually a gallery practice round, they were first designed to fire in barrels mounted outside a main artillery gun or placed in a drill round. The primer is heavily reinforced with a protecting cap that often appears to be either copper or brass, which protects it from the hard blow of an artillery firing pin.

UNITED STATES

Arsenal: Frankford
Philadelphia, Pennsylvania

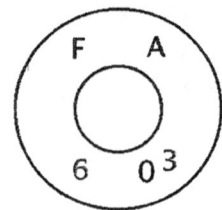

Headstamp

Side View

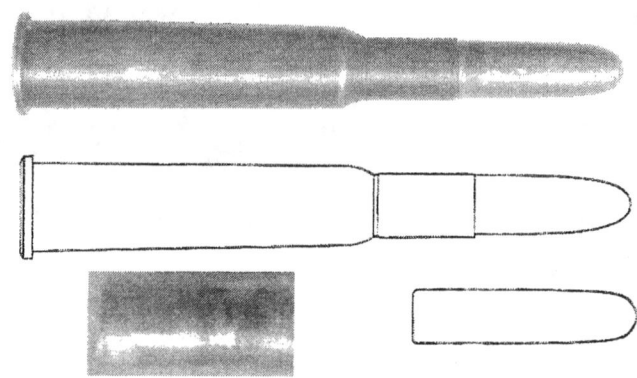

SPECIMEN DIMENSIONS

Rim Measurement: .538
Neck Measurement: .333
Bullet Diameter: .306
Case Length: 2.306

Cole bullet (smooth)

OTHER DETAILS

Caliber: .30-40 Krag
Manufacture Date: 1903
Specialty: Ball
Cartridge Type: Rifle

Overall Length: 3.106

General Information: This cartridge was adapted after many complaints were received about the 3-cannelure bullets lack of accuracy on the range. The Cole bullet was "smooth" or totally void of cannelures and its weight was kept at 220 grains with the cupronickel jacket and lead antimony core whose overall length was 1.366. This cartridge is easily recognized by the seating cannelure on the shoulder of the case. However in 1904 this case type would also be used in a reduced range (gallery) cartridge with a lead projectile.

UNITED STATES

Arsenal: Frankford
Philadelphia, Pennsylvania

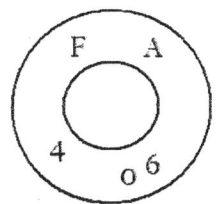

Headstamp

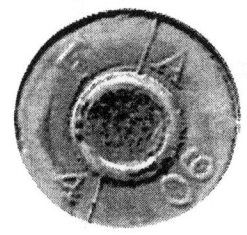

Side View

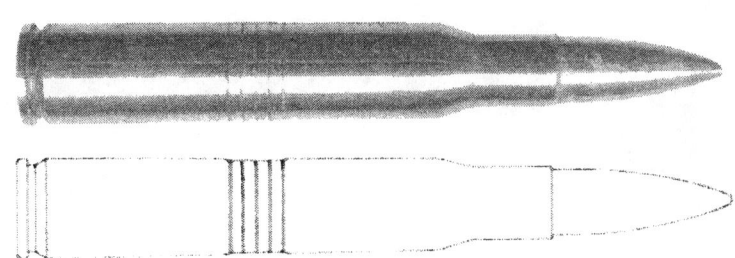

SPECIMEN DIMENSIONS

Rim Measurement: .470
Neck Measurement: .335
Bullet Diameter: .308
Case Length: 2.592

Guard Load Cartridge, Early type

OTHER DETAILS

Caliber: .30 Springfield
Manufacture Date: 1906
Specialty: Guard M1906
Cartridge Type: Rifle

Overall Length: 3.286

General Information: This cartridge known as the Guard M1906 early type can be easily identified by the 5 cannelures encircling the middle of the round and a vertical slash mark cut through the head. The loading for this cartridge consisted of 16.1 grains of Dupont rifle smokeless No. 1 powder. The muzzle velocity for this round was about 1200 f.p.s.

UNITED STATES

Arsenal: Frankford
Philadelphia, Pennsylvania

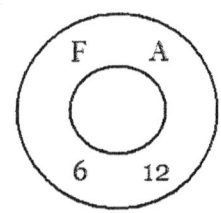

Headstamp   Side View

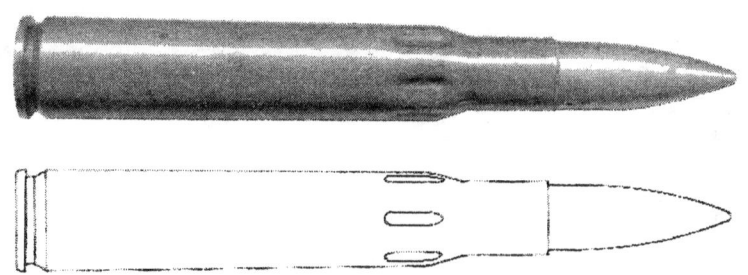

SPECIMEN DIMENSIONS

Rim Measurement: .472
Neck Measurement: .337
Bullet Diameter: .308
Case Length: 2.494

Guard Load Cartridge, Late type

OTHER DETAILS

Caliber: .30 Springfield
Manufacture Date: 1912
Specialty: Guard M 1906
Cartridge Type: Rifle

Overall Length: 3.352

General Information: This cartridge known as the Guard M1906 late type can be easily identified by the 6 lengthwise corrugations on the case shoulder. As existing supplies became depleted, the roll of guard cartridge was often taken over by the M 1919 Gallery practice cartridge.

UNITED STATES

Arsenal: Frankford
Philadelphia, Pennsylvania

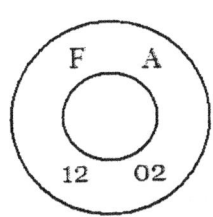

Headstamp

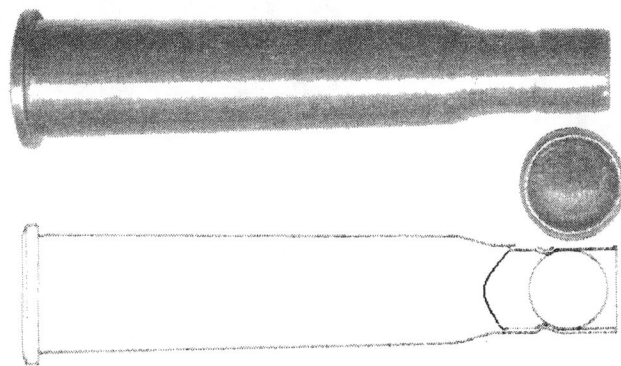

Side View

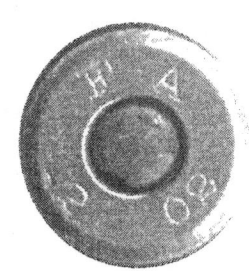

SPECIMEN DIMENSIONS

Rim Measurement: .536
Neck Measurement: .333
Bullet Diameter: .286
Case Length: N/A

Practice Cartridge

OTHER DETAILS

Caliber: .30-40 Krag
Manufacture Date: 1902
Specialty: Practice
Cartridge Type: Rifle

Overall Length: 2.328

General Information: This cartridge is somewhat similar looking to the (2) multiball cartridge used for guard duty. The forward enclosure contains one ball shaped lead projectile made for target practice. However the rifle bore would have to be cleaned thoroughly every 5 shots due to large amounts of residue.

UNITED STATES

Arsenal: Frankford
Philadelphia, Pennsylvania

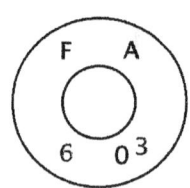

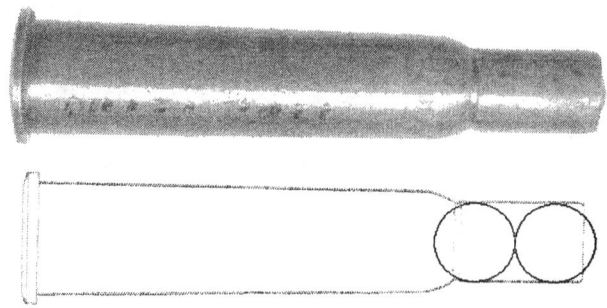

Headstamp

Side View

SPECIMEN DIMENSIONS

Rim Measurement: .536
Neck Measurement: .333
Bullet Diameter: .286
Case Length: 2.306

Guard Load Cartridge

OTHER DETAILS

Caliber: .30-40 Krag
Manufacture Date: 1903
Specialty: Multiball (2)
Cartridge Type: Rifle

Overall Length: 2.328

General Information: This guard load resembles the gallery practice round except for the addition of a second ball and the relocation of the case cannelure holding the multi-ball (2) in place. The production life of this cartridge was short-lived, ending in May of 1904. The next Frankford experiment, a solid 156 grain bullet with a ball behind it never made it to final production, before the ball was eliminated. The label warns that the round will not fit into the rifles magazine as it was designed to be placed directly into the rifles bore one at a time.

UNITED STATES

Arsenal: Frankford
Philadelphia, Pennsylvania

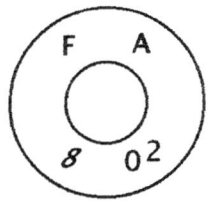

Headstamp

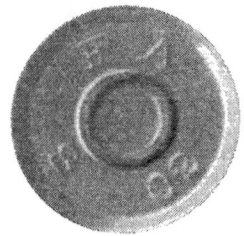

Side View

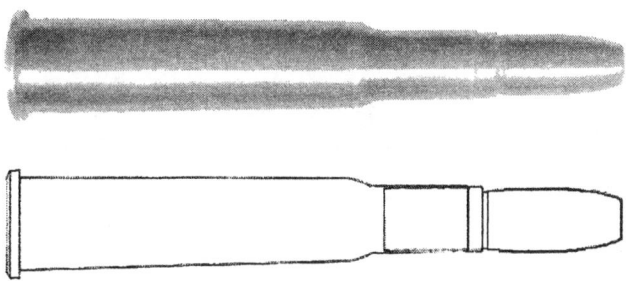

SPECIMEN DIMENSIONS

Rim Measurement: .536
Neck Measurement: .338
Bullet Diameter: .320
Case Length: 2.298

Experimental Cartridge?

OTHER DETAILS

Caliber: .30-40 Krag
Manufacture Date: 1902
Specialty: Unknown
Cartridge Type: Rifle

Overall Length: 3.108

General Information: Is this cartridge an experimental round developed in August of 1902 an attempt to improve the seal, bullet pull or accuracy of gallery ammunition? The single cannelure solid lead (flat based/flat tipped) bullet measured 1.320. I have no doubt that all collectors have at least one cartridge that defies definitive identification. I call this specimen my bottle stopper cartridge because of it's obvious form.

UNITED STATES

Arsenal: Frankford
Philadelphia, Pennsylvania

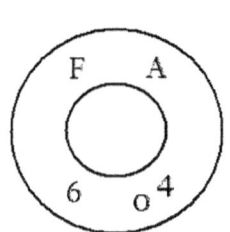

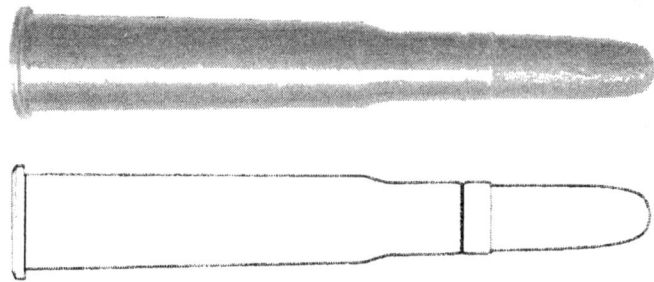

Headstamp

Side View

SPECIMEN DIMENSIONS

Rim Measurement: .538
Neck Measurement: .335
Bullet Diameter: .305
Case Length: 2.307

Guard Load Cartridge

OTHER DETAILS

Caliber: .30-40 Krag
Manufacture Date: 1904
Specialty: Guard
Cartridge Type: Rifle

Overall Length: 3.81

General Information: This cartridge is yet another variation of the guard cartridge with a reduced powder load reportedly accurate between 100 and 200 yards. Its bullet is has a combination of lead and tin, giving it an odd texture. The powder charge was found to be approximately 14 grains, which kept the muzzle velocity beneath the usual 1200 f.p.s. for a guard round.

UNITED STATES

Arsenal: Frankford
Philadelphia, Pennsylvania

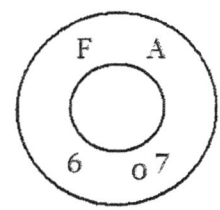

Headstamp

Side View

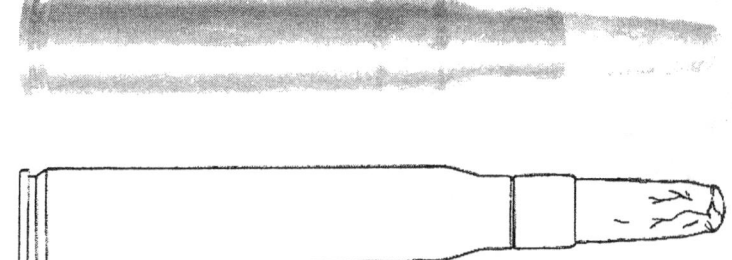

SPECIMEN DIMENSIONS

Rim Measurement: .538
Neck Measurement: .336
Bullet Diameter: 285
Case Length: 2.485

Blank cartridge

OTHER DETAILS

Caliber: .30 Springfield
Manufacture Date: 1907
Specialty: Blank M 1903
Cartridge Type: Rifle

Overall Length: 3.252

General Information: This blank cartridge was made with a stannic wash or tinned case and a copper primer. The paper bullet contains powder sealed with shellac and then coated with paraffin. The main powder charge inside the case amounts to 10 grains total. A single cannelure seats the paper bullet .272 behind the case mouth. The purpose of this cartridge is largely ceremonial.

UNITED STATES

Arsenal: Frankford
Philadelphia, Pennsylvania

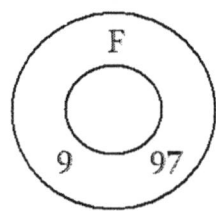

Headstamp

Side View

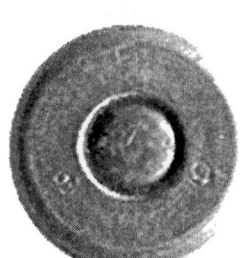

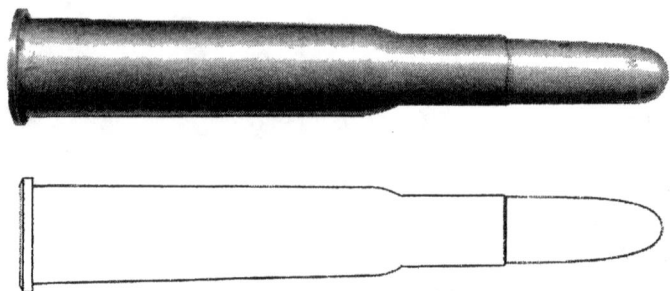

SPECIMEN DIMENSIONS

Rim Measurement: .540
Neck Measurement: .334
Bullet Diameter: .305
Case Length: 2.308

Tinned case & primer

OTHER DETAILS

Caliber: .30–40 Krag
Manufacture Date: 1897
Specialty: Ball
Cartridge Type: Rifle

Overall Length: 3.164

General Information: This tinned brass cased specimen also has a tinned brass primer cup. Is this the result of an 1894 practice to counter the effects of fulminate of mercury, which weakened plain brass primer cups to the point it made them susceptible to accidental firing? There would be a partial return to plain brass primer cups in 1896 after a minor modification to rifle firing pins. Notice the F on the headstamp denoting the Frankford Arsenal headstamp identification code, the (A) in more familiar (F A) would not be added to the bunter until July of 1902.

UNITED STATES

Arsenal: Union Metallic Cartridge
Bridgeport, Connecticut

Headstamp

Side View

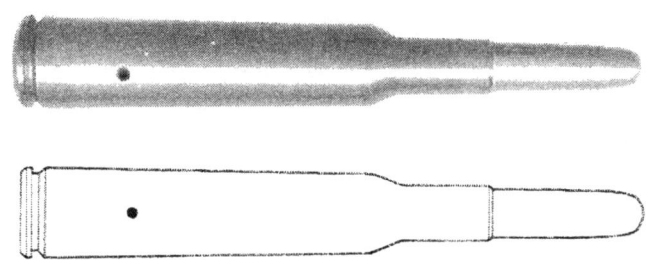

SPECIMEN DIMENSIONS

Rim Measurement: .446
Neck Measurement: .274
Bullet Diameter: .236
Case Length: 2.348

.236 United States Navy

OTHER DETAILS

Caliber: .236
Manufacture Date: c1898
Specialty: Dummy
Cartridge Type: Rifle

Overall Length: 3.2

General Information: The "Lee Navy" cartridge began being manufactured about 1894 after its initial period of experimentation by Winchester. Dummy cartridges can be found with tinned gilding metal or cupronickel-plated steel bullets and nickel, brass or copper primer cups. They all have a wooden spacer inside the case to keep the bullet forward but UMC put the case hole nearest the head while Winchester placed theirs near the shoulder.

The majority of these rounds are marked with the .236 U.S.N headstamp although a smaller number were marked 6 M/M U.S.N. Testing versions sported a 135 grain bullet before the offically adapted 112 grain bullet became the standard to the Lee straight pull rifle and the Winchester model 1895. In 1898 a Navy contract for 50,000 dummy rounds was equally split between Winchester and Union Metallic.

UNITED STATES

Arsenal: Winchester Repeating Arms Company
New Haven, Connecticut

Headstamp   Side View

   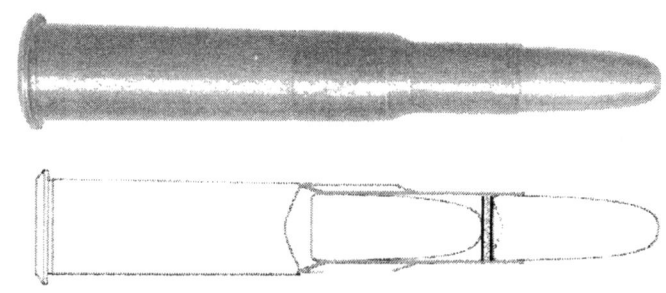

SPECIMEN DIMENSIONS

Rim Measurement: .536
Neck Measurement: .333
Bullet Diameter: .286
Case Length: 2.306

R.W. Scott Multiball Guard / Riot Cartridge

OTHER DETAILS

Caliber: .30-40 Krag
Manufacture Date: 1900
Specialty: Multiball (2)
Cartridge Type: Rifle

Overall Length: 2.328

General Information: This two bullet (120 grains each) was designed to increase chances of striking the target but at the same time being less lethal at low velocity. A sleeve over the case brings the overall size back to standard. Besides the main powder charge there is also an in-between charge to insure separation of the projectiles in flight. A three-bullet (77 grains each) model was also tested and is similar in function but the projectile size is noticeably smaller. This cartridge would prove to be short lived as it was replaced by the double ball design in 1902.

UNITED STATES

Arsenal: Frankford
Philadelphia, Pennsylvania

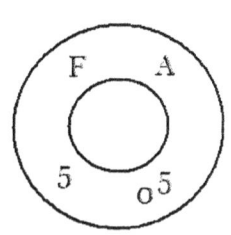 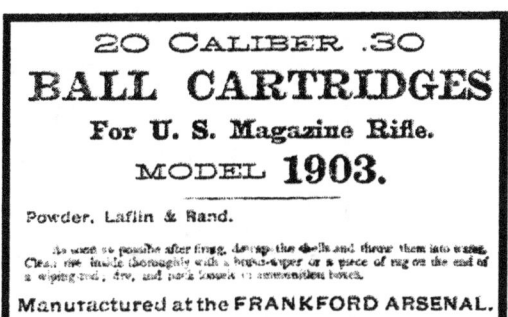

Headstamp   Side View

 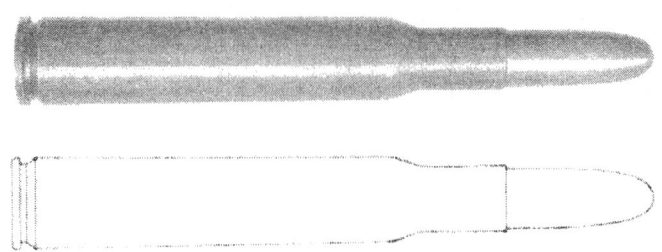

SPECIMEN DIMENSIONS

Rim Measurement: .470
Neck Measurement: .336
Bullet Diameter: .307
Case Length: 2.492

Model 1903 Ball

OTHER DETAILS

Caliber: .30
Manufacture Date: 1905
Specialty: Ball
Cartridge Type: Rifle / MG

Overall Length: 3.374

General Information: This cartridge was made to fit the magazines of the new 1903 Springfield rifle. It has a rimless case and a greater velocity then the .30-40 Krag.

However, in September of 1905 the powder load was reduced to lower the velocity from 2,300 fps to 2,200 fps to prolong barrel life. The specimen pictured above was made in May of 1905 and therefore contains the larger powder load producing 2,300 fps. All previously existing rounds of this higher powder load were supposed to have been reloaded to the correct amount and a line cut across the bass of each round to signify the procedure had been done. Again, this specimen does not have the cut and therefore must have slipped out or shipped out prior to the conversion.

UNITED STATES

Arsenal: Frankford
Philadelphia, Pennsylvania

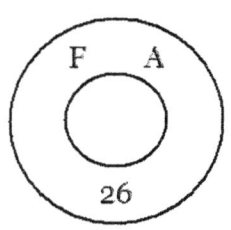

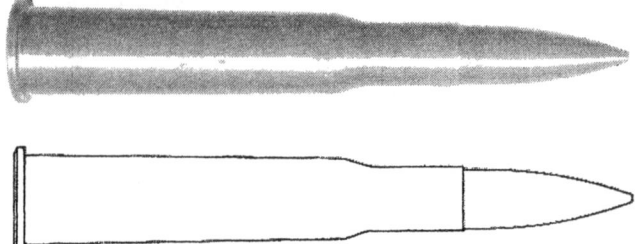

Headstamp

Side View

SPECIMEN DIMENSIONS

Rim Measurement: .537
Neck Measurement: .332
Bullet Diameter: .308
Case Length: 2.318

Sub-Caliber Coastal Artillery Drill Cartridge

OTHER DETAILS

Caliber: .30
Manufacture Date: 1926
Specialty: Sub-Caliber Ball
Cartridge Type: Rifle

Overall Length: 3.276

General Information: The primary function of this cartridge (Model 1925) was to be used in the subcaliber tube of the 3-inch seacoast gun batteries during gallery practice. This round has a reinforced primer cup to withstand the heavy force of an artillery firing pin, much like earlier versions. This cartridge also fit the 1898 Krag rifle, so many were given away to gun clubs when Krag ammunition became less available, a practice which greatly reduced their number.

UNITED STATES

Arsenal: Remington Arms
Hoboken, New Jersey

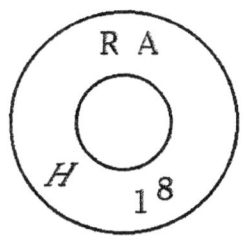

Headstamp

Side View

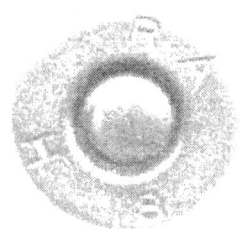

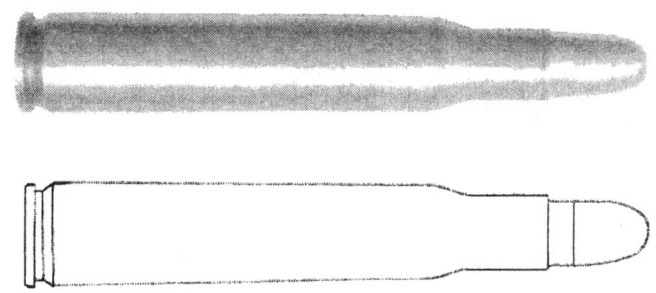

SPECIMEN DIMENSIONS

Rim Measurement: .466
Neck Measurement: .332
Bullet Diameter: .310
Case Length: 2.492

OTHER DETAILS

Caliber: .30 Springfield
Manufacture Date: 1918
Specialty: Practice
Cartridge Type: Rifle

Gallery Practice Round (WW I era)

General Information: This Model 1906 gallery practice round was originally of strict design standards but the increased demands caused by WW I meant that tolerances would become more relaxed and varied between manufacturers in order to prevent delays in production. The H on the head stamp shown above signifies that this specimen was manufactured at the Hoboken, New Jersey facility of Remington Arms. Had the head stamp read (RA and the date), its place of manufacture would have been Bridgeport, Connecticut. Some limited quantities of this cartridge was also produced in Swanton, Vermont with a head stamp of (RA S and the date).

UNITED STATES

Arsenal: Springfield Armory
          Springfield, Massachusetts

Headstamp

Side View

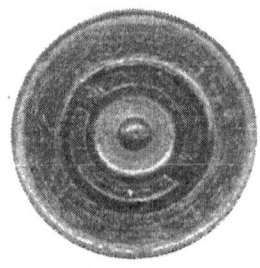
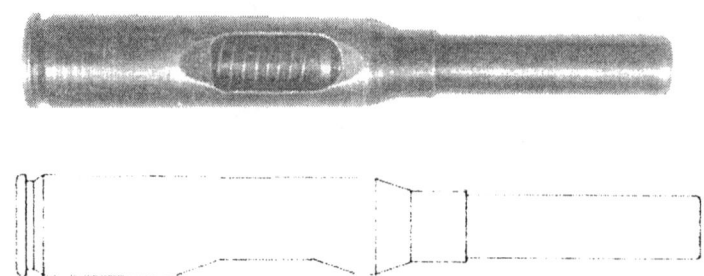

SPECIMEN DIMENSIONS

Rim Measurement: .473
Neck Measurement: .340
Bullet Diameter: N/A
Case Length: N/A

OTHER DETAILS

Caliber: N/A
Manufacture Date: 1907-1919
Specialty: Chamber insert
Cartridge Type: Rifle

Hoffer-Thompson chamber insert

General Information: By inserting this device into the chamber of their service rifle, soldiers could easily convert to .22 cartridges for gallery practice. About 82,000 of these devices would be produced by Springfield Arsenal. Each one being made of machined steel and blued finish. The original device was designed by Maj. Jay E. Hoffer and modified by Maj. J. T. Thompson before production started in January of 1907 at Springfield Arsenal.

Western	June	1918	40,000,000	.22 Short
Remington	July	1918	86,550,000	.22 Short
U.S.C. Co.	August	1918	10,000,000	.22 Short
Winchester	November	1918	10,000,000	.22 Short
Remington	December	1918	2,500,000	.22 Short
Western	December	1918	15,700,000	.22 Short
Peters	June	1919	30,000,000	.22 Short
Remington	July	1918	500,000	.22 Long Rifle
Winchester	August	1918	500,000	.22 Long Rifle

UNITED STATES

Arsenal: Remington Arms
          Bridgeport, Connecticut

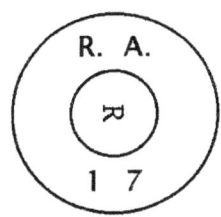

Headstamp

Side View

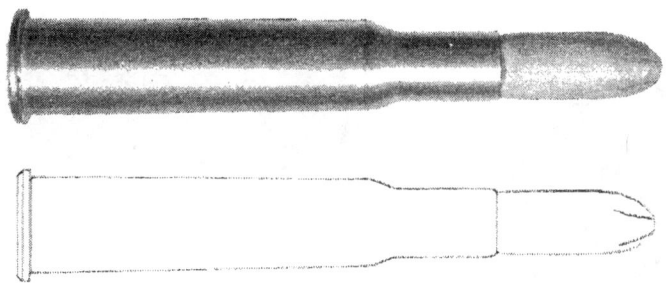

SPECIMEN DIMENSIONS

Rim Measurement: .538
Neck Measurement: .331
Bullet Diameter: 304
Case Length: 2.309

Blank M2 Training Cartridge

OTHER DETAILS

Caliber: .30-40 Krag
Manufacture Date: 1917
Specialty: Blank
Cartridge Type: Rifle

General Information: This blank cartridge was made with a tinned brass case and a yellow waxed paper bullet, used for military training purposes during WWI. The Remington Arms Company fulfilled their U.S. Navy contract for 200,000 rounds over the two-year period of 1917 & 1918.

UNITED STATES

Arsenal: Remington – Union Metallic Cartridge
Bridgeport, Connecticut

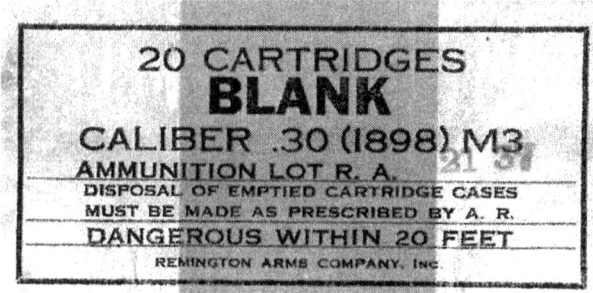

Headstamp   Side View

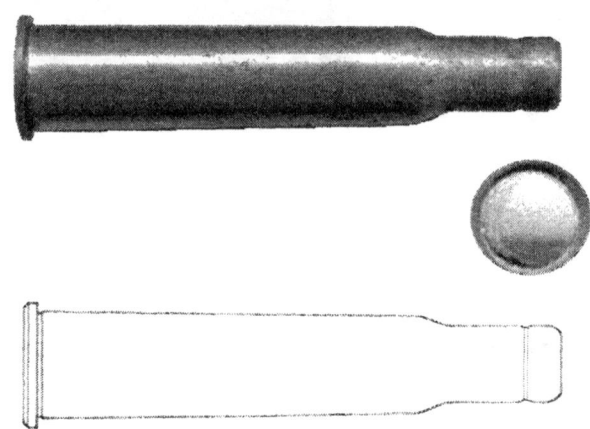

SPECIMEN DIMENSIONS

Rim Measurement: .470
Neck Measurement: .335
Bullet Diameter: N/A
Case Length: 2.49

Blank M3 Cartridge "White"

OTHER DETAILS

Caliber: .30-40 Krag
Manufacture Date: c1930s
Specialty: Blank
Cartridge Type: Rifle

General Information: This model 1898 blank (M3) cartridge which enclosed 5 grains of EC powder behind a varnished white paper disc was primarily used for ceremonies. This specimen came from the box pictured above, which was unsealed for this occasion.

UNITED STATES

Arsenal: National Conduit & Cable Co,
Hastings on the Hudson, New York

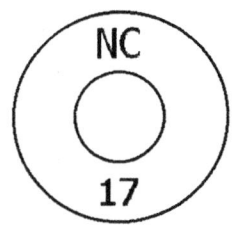

Headstamp

Side View

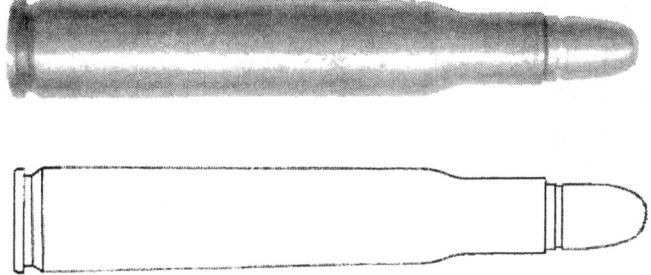

SPECIMEN DIMENSIONS

Rim Measurement: .466
Neck Measurement: .335
Bullet Diameter: .310
Case Length: 2.472

Gallery Practice

OTHER DETAILS

Caliber: .30 Springfield
Manufacture Date: 1917
Specialty: Gallery Practice
Cartridge Type: Rifle / MG

Overall Length: 2.940

General Information: This Model 1906 practice round was produced by National Conduit and Cable Co. In 1917 this firm was given a Navy contract for 30 million rounds of cal .30 Model 1906 ball ammunition. In total 22,700,000 were actually produced and delivered, but all of them were found to be unsatisfactory by the United States Navy which subsequently withdrew them from service. Nearly bankrupt, the company changed their name to National Brass and Copper Tube Co. in 1918 and secured additional contracts that were successfully concluded using the head stamp CNI.

UNITED STATES

Arsenal: Remington Arms
Bridgeport, Connecticut

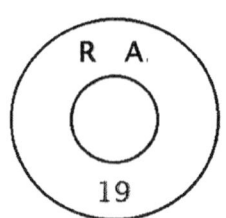

Headstamp

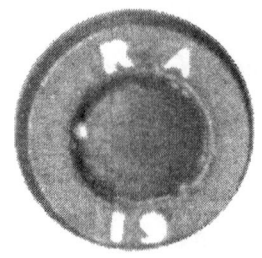

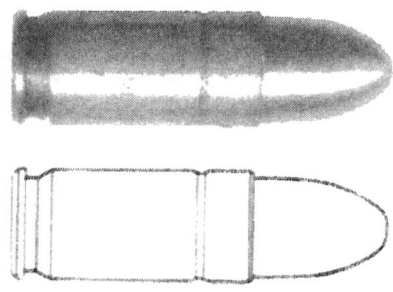

Side View

200 CAL .30 AUTO.
PISTOL BALL CARTRIDGES
MODEL OF 1918
THE REMINGTON ARMS
UNION METALLIC CARTRIDGE COMPANY, INC.
BRIDGEPORT, CONN.

Reproduction

SPECIMEN DIMENSIONS

Rim Measurement: .332
Neck Measurement: .335
Bullet Diameter: 309
Case Length: .779

.30 -18 (Pederson Device Ammunition)

OTHER DETAILS

Caliber: .30 Auto
Manufacture Date:1919
Specialty: Ball M 1918
Cartridge Type: Rifle

Overall Length: 1.200

General Information: This cartridge was produced to be used with the Pederson device (1917) which was secretly made to convert the model 1903 rifle into a semi-automatic assault weapon for use in trench warfare. However, due to the ending of WWI the device was never issued in any numbers. Some 1903 Springfield rifles have a square access slot cut into the sidewall of the receiver, which is where the device would be attached and replaced the bolt. The Pederson device itself is so scarce they have been known to sell in excess of $20,000 dollars without the rifle. The cartridge pictured above features a smooth cannelure and a tinned bullet. Past problems included extractor trouble and case rupturing which lead to the increased sidewall thickness of this model.

UNITED STATES

Arsenal: Frankford
Philadelphia, Pennsylvania

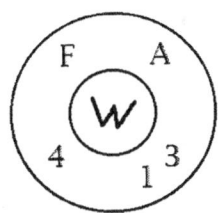

Headstamp

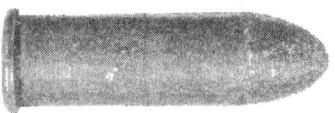

Side View

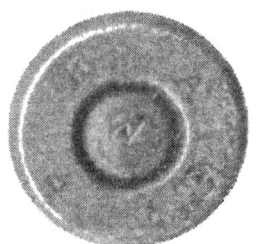

SPECIMEN DIMENSIONS

Rim Measurement: .436
Neck Measurement: N/a
Bullet Diameter: .369
Case Length: 1.18

.38 Long Colt Revolver

OTHER DETAILS

Caliber: .38 Long Colt
Manufacture Date: 1913
Specialty: Ball
Cartridge Type: Revolver

Overall Length: 1.366

General Information: The .38 Colt was the official revolver cartridge of the United States Army & Navy until it was replaced by the .45 automatic in 1911. The experience gained during several period conflicts (Spanish-American War) emphasized the need to increase side arm stopping power.

This specimen has a "Navy style" bullet (pointed) and although it is slightly discolored, you can readily make out the case seating cannelure, which is positioned "Army style". I have not found any explanation for the seemingly combined style components of this specimen from the 1913 period. The last known loading was at the Frankford arsenal in March of 1915. Other headstamps encountered are W.R.A. Co., P.C. Co., U.S.C. Co. and REM-UMC.

UNITED STATES

Arsenal: Frankford
Philadelphia, Pennsylvania

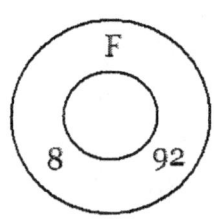

Headstamp

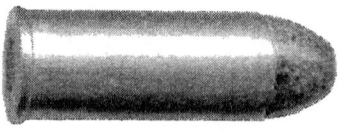

Side View

SPECIMEN DIMENSIONS

Rim Measurement: .518
Neck Measurement: .476
Bullet Diameter: .442
Case Length: 1.108

.45 Revolver

OTHER DETAILS

Caliber: .45 Revolver
Manufacture Date: 1892
Specialty: Ball
Cartridge Type: Revolver

Overall Length: 1.422

General Information: This cartridge was the first series to be re-designated revolver cartridge as opposed to pistol. The earlier 1882 cartridges had copper cases while this specimen dated 1892 has a tinned brass case. About 1886 the letter R was ordered to be added to the headstamp bunter (R F 5 93).

Experimentation with revolver projectiles included one that had two smaller projectiles behind the main bullet submitted by Merwin Hulbert of New York and another single divided bullet cross cut into four sections submitted by Dr. L. B. Anderson of Norfolk, Virginia. Unfortunately, at the conclusion of testing conducted at the Springfield arsenal, both designs had a dispersion radius too great to hit anything and their ability to penetrate targets was also lacking.

UNITED STATES

Arsenal: Frankford
Philadelphia, Pennsylvania

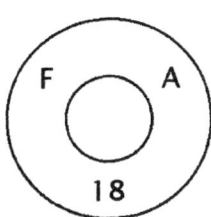

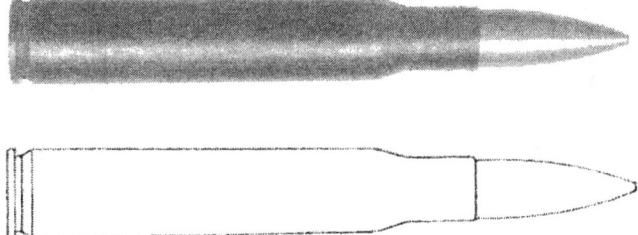

Headstamp

Side View

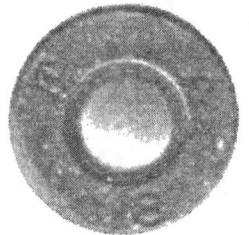

SPECIMEN DIMENSIONS

Rim Measurement: .468
Neck Measurement: .338
Bullet Diameter: .308
Case Length: 2.498

Type Used During WW I

OTHER DETAILS

Caliber: 30-06
Manufacture Date: 1918
Specialty: Tracer
Cartridge Type: Aircraft MG only

Overall Length: 3.318

General Information: This tracer round was oddly enough made to be readily identifiable by its blackened case, a method of identification never before or since used by the U.S. military. The pre-primed cases were soaked in a solution of sodium hyposulphide, lead acetate and boiling water for 5 minutes and then rinsed. 1918 was the first year of manufacture for this type of process, which would continue until 1930. Varying tracer igniters including red, green and white were also experimented with and denoted on the round by adding colored shellac at the base or a stripe at the tip. This was the beginning of the modern method of color code identification.

UNITED STATES

Arsenal: Frankford
          Philadelphia, Pennsylvania

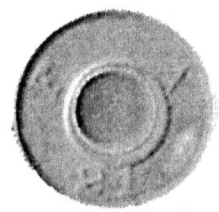

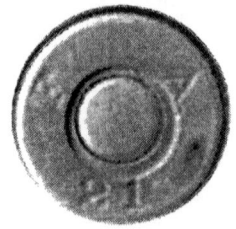

Headstamp   Side View

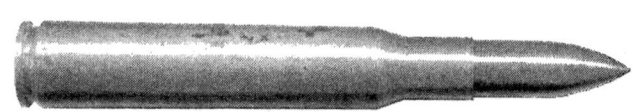

SPECIMEN DIMENSIONS

Rim Measurement: .468
Neck Measurement: .338
Bullet Diameter: .308
Case Length: 2.498

Experimental

OTHER DETAILS

Caliber: .30-06
Manufacture Date: 1921
Specialty: Unknown
Cartridge Type: Unkown

Overall Length: 3.318

General Information: Armor piercing rounds of various caliber's were tested during the 1917 - 1932 period. Many shapes and metals were tested in an attempt to match form with function to produce varied levels of penetration. This specimen with its distinctive ogive shape matches one described in a Frankford Arsenal 1920 concept drawing that was produced in limited quantity for testing at the Aberdeen proving ground. However, the projectile failed the magnet test indicating there is no steel core present. It does has a copper jacket and I assume a lead core. I am reluctant to pull the bullet since it is the only one in my possession or ever seen for that matter. Since rigorous experimentation was also conducted on National match ammunition around this same period one can only speculate about the possibilities. The opportunity for discovery is what makes this interesting.

UNITED STATES

Arsenal: Frankford
Philadelphia, Pennsylvania

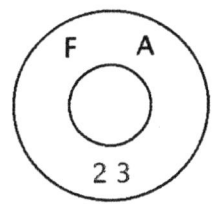

Headstamp

Side View

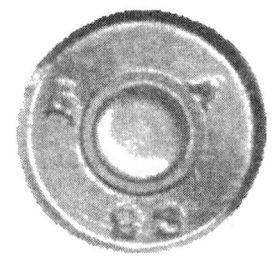

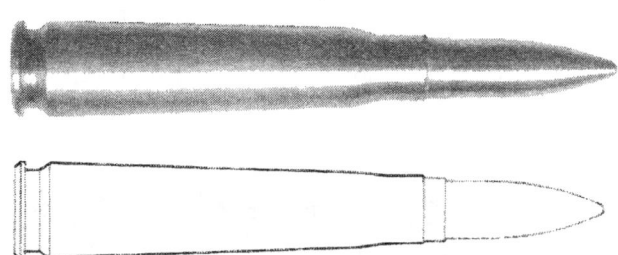

SPECIMEN DIMENSIONS

Rim Measurement: .450
Neck Measurement: .309
Bullet Diameter: .289
Case Length: 1.902

Pederson Ball Cartridge

OTHER DETAILS

Caliber: .276
Manufacture Date: 1923
Specialty: Ball Bronze
Cartridge Type: Rifle

Overall Length: 2.815

General Information: In 1923 J.D. Pederson was awarded an army contract to build his proposed semi automatic rifle at the Springfield Armory while at the same time develop a caliber .276 cartridge at Frankford Arsenal under the supervision of Major J. S. Hatcher.

This cartridge can be identified as the original bullet type (SK-299) bronze with an early case CC-1 (notice extreme angle of taper) and a monel-metal primer cup. The first few cartridges were practically hand made, but by October of 1923 there were 1,500 produced.

UNITED STATES

Arsenal: Frankford
Philadelphia, Pennsylvania

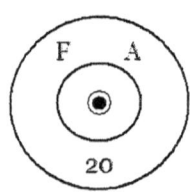

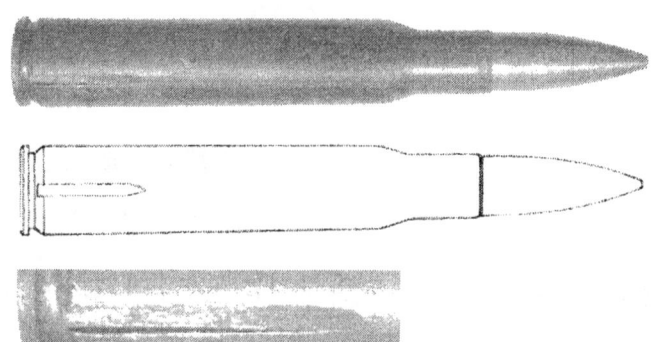

Headstamp

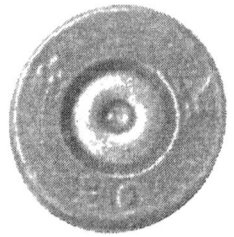

Side View

DIMENSIONS

Rim Measurement: .466
Neck Measurement: .334
Bullet Diameter: .308
Case Length: 2.495

Range Dummy

OTHER DETAILS

Caliber: .30 M 1903
Manufacture Date: 1920-25
Specialty: Range Dummy
Cartridge Type: Rifle

Overall Length: 3.316

General Information: This odd looking round can be identified by a square vertical cut made into the case from the extractor groove to .585 forward. This cartridge was introduced about 1925 but earlier dates may be encountered on the headstamps due to the reuse of brass cases. This specimen also had 3 groves all the way around the rear of the bullet in a cork screw pattern.

UNITED STATES

Arsenal: Frankford
Philadelphia, Pennsylvania

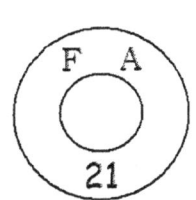

Headstamp

Side View

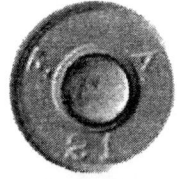

A.

B.

SPECIMEN DIMENSIONS

Rim Measurement: .450
Neck Measurement: .309
Bullet Diameter: .289
Case Length: 1.902

Aircraft Ball MG Cartridge

OTHER DETAILS

Caliber: .30
Manufacture Date: 1921
Specialty: Ball M06
Cartridge Type: A/MG

Overall Length: 2.815

General Information: This 1921 Ball round (specimen "A") taken from a box marked "For aircraft use" Model of 1906 has no markings on the round itself to indicate this special purpose. However, it remains a good example of the original type of aircraft ball round (circa 1917) that would encounter "blow out" problems.

It would be decided in 1918 by some companies to add a heavy primer ring with stab crimps (specimen "B") to prevent primers from "blowing out" as the problem was reported due to excessive bolt strike in aircraft machine guns. Specimen "B" also shows the design modifications by U.S.C. Co. using the new "Hooker extruded process" signified by the stars on either side of the headstamp. This enabled the manufacture to produce cartridges faster and with fewer steps although this process proved to be more costly. In later years firing pins would be made differently and existing ones replaced.

UNITED STATES

Arsenal: Frankford
Philadelphia, Pennsylvania

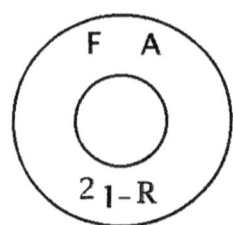

```
┌─────────────────────────────────┐
│         20 CARTRIDGES           │
│     BALL CALIBER .30M1          │
│     1921 NATIONAL MATCH         │
│            IN CLIPS             │
│         LOT NUMBER 672          │
├─────────────────────────────────┤
│ DISPOSAL OF EMPTIED CASES MUST BE│
│ MADE AS PRESCRIBED BY A.R.      │
├─────────────────────────────────┤
│ Manufactured by FRANKFORD ARSENAL│
└─────────────────────────────────┘
```
Reproduction

Headstamp

Side View

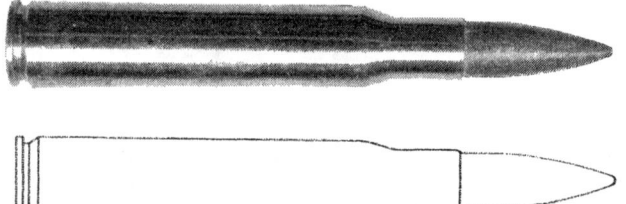

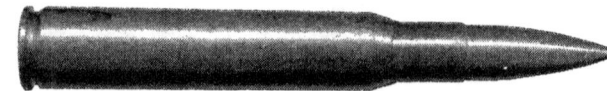

DIMENSIONS

Rim Measurement: .468
Neck Measurement: .332
Bullet Diameter: .340
Case Length: 2.590

National Match Ammunition

OTHER DETAILS

Caliber: .30
Manufacture Date: 1921
Specialty: Match Ball
Cartridge Type: Rifle

Overall Length: 3.30

General Information: This is the infamous "Tin Can", the bullet was tin-plated to reduce metal fouling and a chemical reaction between the tin and the case neck caused excessive bullet pull. Despite warnings to the contrary some cartridges were greased and thus resulted in blown rifle barrels at the National matches. This specimen may have been one of the tinned gilding metal-jacketed bullets as you can barely see the remnants of this material. Both crimped and non-crimped primers are known from various specimens. Later years would have the letters NM for National Match, I&P International Match (1927-1929) and P or PM for Palma Match.

UNITED STATES

Arsenal: Frankford
Philadelphia, Pennsylvania

Union Metallic Cartridge Co.
Bridgeport, Connecticut

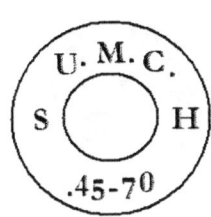

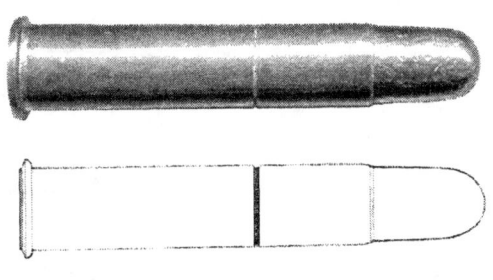

Headstamp

Side View

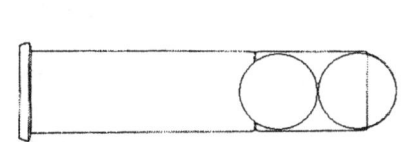

GALLERY   MULTIBALL

SPECIMEN DIMENSIONS

Rim Measurement: .603
Neck Measurement: .581
Bullet Diameter: .450
Case Length: 2.105

.45 – 70 Ball

OTHER DETAILS

Caliber: .45-70
Manufacture Date: 1902
Specialty: Ball, Black Powder
Cartridge Type: Rifle

Overall Length: 2.738

General Information: Although the headstamp clearly indicates this cartridge was made at Union Metallic Cartridge Company, it was "assembled" at Frankford Arsenal on a contract deal between the two firms. Seven million rounds of this type were produced by various commercial contracts during the Spanish – American War. In 1917 (WWI) the .45 caliber rifle was issued to second line defense units and installations. Many cases were reloaded for this purpose including both ball, gallery and multiball cartridges.

UNITED STATES

Arsenal: Frankford
Philadelphia, Pennsylvania

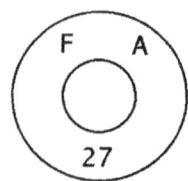

Headstamp

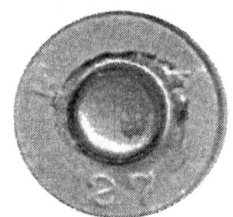

Side View

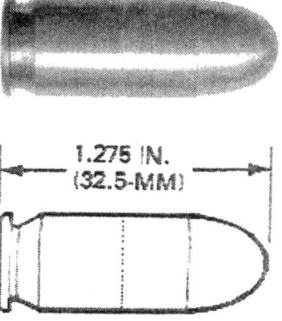

SPECIMEN DIMENSIONS

Rim Measurement: .468
Neck Measurement: N/a
Bullet Diameter: .438
Case Length: .891

.45 Automatic Pistol

OTHER DETAILS

Caliber: .45
Manufacture Date: 1927
Specialty: Ball
Cartridge Type: Pistol

Overall Length: 1.275

General Information: Advancement in bullet pull technology is evident when you examine earlier specimens with such heavy bullet seating cannelures.

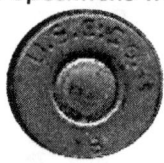

In 1917 U S C Co. added three stab crimps above the smooth seating cannelure to keep the bullet from moving forward. During this same year the American Expeditionary Forces in Europe also reported primer ignition problems which caused production to halt around June of 1918.

Note: Winchester 1918 Headstamp variation of either a large or small (W) (w) are known to exist.

UNITED STATES

Arsenal: Frankford
Philadelphia, Pennsylvania

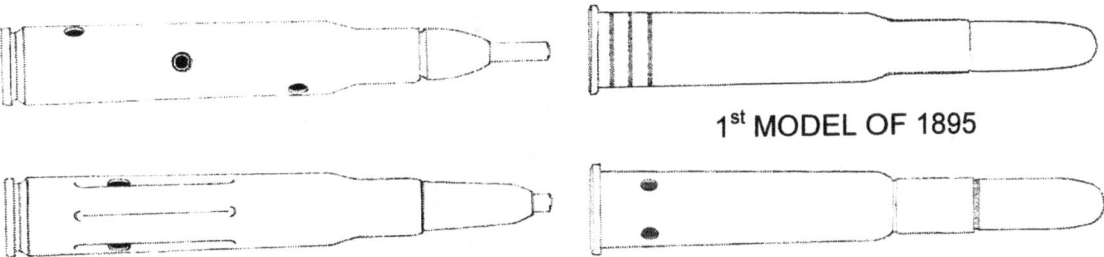

1st MODEL OF 1895

MODEL 1906 Hollifield Dotter

2nd MODEL OF 1895

Headstamp

Side View

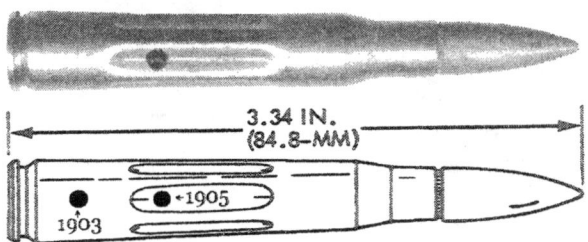

SPECIMEN DIMENSIONS

Rim Measurement: .469
Neck Measurement: .334
Bullet Diameter: .308
Case Length: 2.486

Dummy / Practice cartridges

OTHER DETAILS

Caliber: .30
Manufacture Date: 1933
Specialty: Dummy
Cartridge Type: Dummy

Overall Length: 3.34

General Information: Dummy cartridges are primarily used for practice or to test the function of rifle/mg actions and magazines. This specimen was re-made from a tinned case and primer. Cases can be found with or without holes. The original 1903 model had 4 holes located before the corrugations toward the rim, however problems arose when it was reported that the holes kept catching on the ejector mechanism, so the holes were relocated forward within the corrugations around 1905.

Earlier models of dummy cartridges such as the top right pair for the Krag rifle was among the first examples using tactile markings.

Practice cartridges like the unique Hollifield Dotter System (top left pair) came in a kit form and was manufactured by the Hollifield Practice Rod Co. of Middletown, New York.

UNITED STATES

Arsenal: Twin Cities Ordnance Plant
Minneapolis, Minnesota

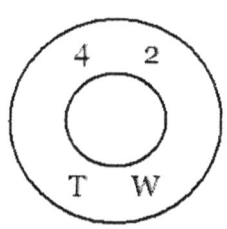

Headstamp

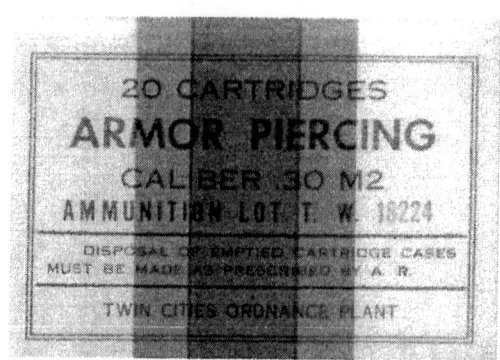

Side View

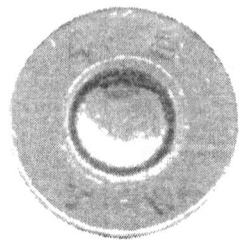

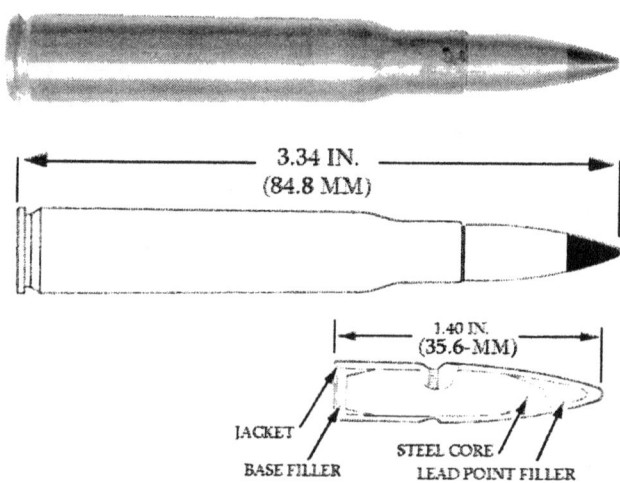

DIMENSIONS

Rim Measurement: .466
Neck Measurement: .332
Bullet Diameter: .308
Case Length: 2.476

Armor Piercing M2

OTHER DETAILS

Caliber: .30 M2
Manufacture Date: 1942
Specialty: AP
Cartridge Type: Rifle / Mg

General Information: The Federal Cartridge Co. from 1941 to 1945 operated this plant during WWII. It was one of the largest volume producers of .30 – .45 – .50 caliber ammunition.

UNITED STATES

Arsenal: Frankford
Philadelphia, Pennsylvania

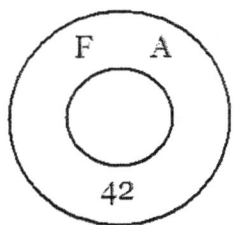

Headstamp

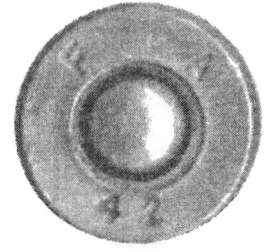

Side View

SPECIMEN DIMENSIONS

Rim Measurement: .468
Neck Measurement: .335
Bullet Diameter: N/A
Case Length: N/A

Grenade Blank used during World War II

OTHER DETAILS

Caliber: .30 Springfield
Manufacture Date: 1942
Specialty: Grenade, M3
Cartridge Type: Rifle

Overall Length: 2.484

General Information: Not to be confused with a blank cartridge, this grenade round was used as an ignition source for the rifle grenades of the period. The 5 petal crimps enclose a paper wad sealed with red lacquer. The powder load was measured at around 50 grains.

UNITED STATES

Arsenal: Twin Cities Ordnance Plant
Minneapolis, Minnesota

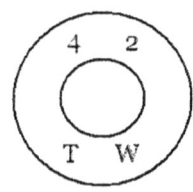

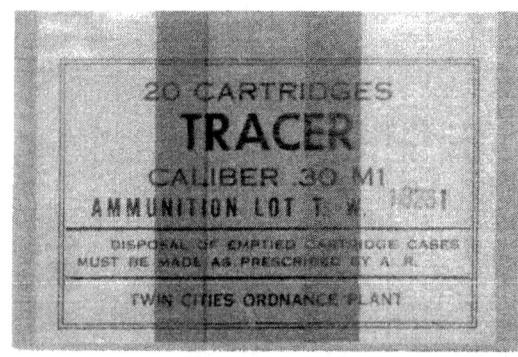

Headstamp

Side View

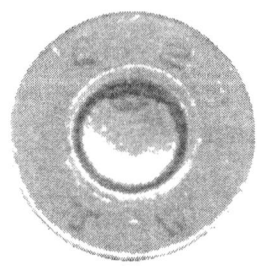

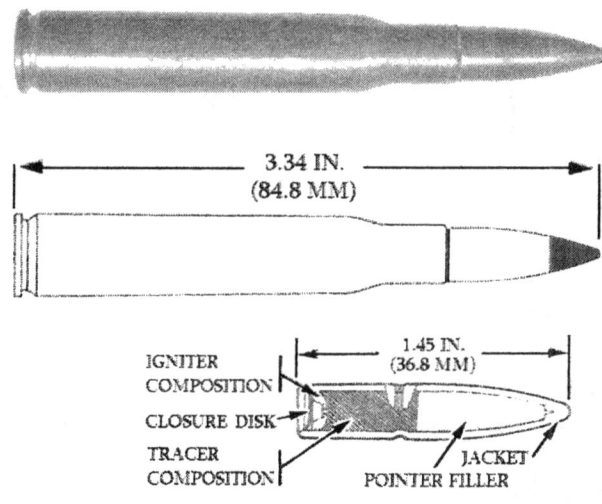

DIMENSIONS

Rim Measurement: .468
Neck Measurement: .335
Bullet Diameter: .308
Case Length: 2.480

Tracer M1

OTHER DETAILS

Caliber: .30
Manufacture Date: 1942
Specialty: Tracer
Cartridge Type: Rifle / Mg

General Information: The Federal Cartridge Company operated this plant from 1941 – 1945. This plant would also operate during future conflicts as well.

UNITED STATES

Arsenal: Eau Claire Ordnance Plant
Eau Claire, Wisconsin

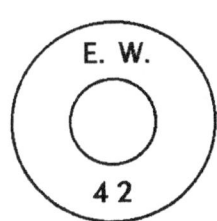

Headstamp

Side View

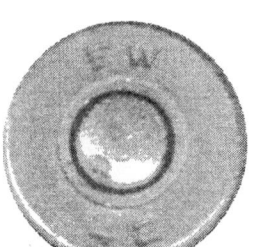

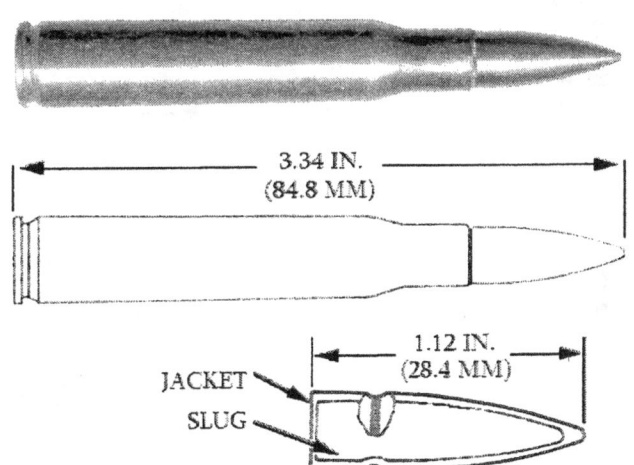

SPECIMEN DIMENSIONS

Rim Measurement: .468
Neck Measurement: .338
Bullet Diameter: .308
Case Length: 2.481

Ball M2 adapted in 1938

OTHER DETAILS

Caliber: .30
Manufacture Date: 1942
Specialty: Ball
Cartridge Type: Rifle / MG

General Information: This plant was operated by the U.S. Rubber Co. from 1942 to 1943 which only produced .30 caliber ammunition. The fabled E C head stamp was only used for the first few production lots before it was changed to E.W. to avoid confusion with Evansville.

UNITED STATES

Arsenal: Evansville-Chrysler
Evansville, Indiana

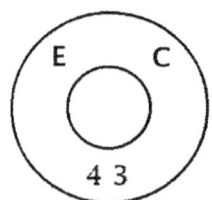

Headstamp

Side View

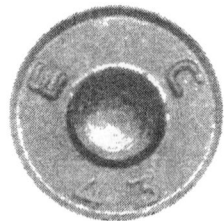

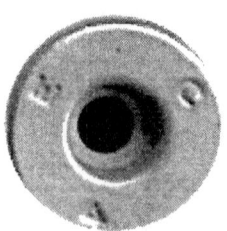

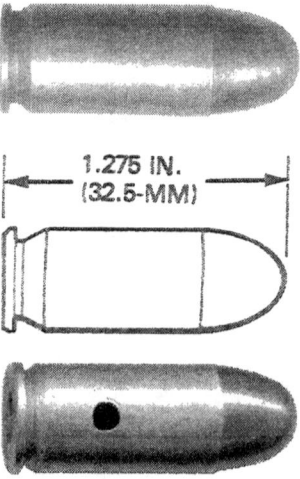

SPECIMEN DIMENSIONS

Rim Measurement: .468
Neck Measurement: 442
Bullet Diameter: .438
Case Length: .891

OTHER DETAILS

Caliber: .45
Manufacture Date: 1943/44
Specialty: Ball
Cartridge Type: Pistol

.45 Steel Case Pistol Ball & Dummy Round (Lacquered)

General Information: This steel cased lacquered round produced during the war years has a box label (pictured above) that states it was repacked in July of 1944 for what reasons we can only speculate. Below that round is a dummy cartridge also made by E C in 1944. The single 4 on the headstamp was a cost cutting measure to limit expense on the headstamp bunter.

UNITED STATES

Arsenal: Twin Cities Ordnance Plant
Minneapolis, Minnesota

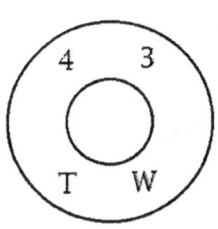

Headstamp

Side View

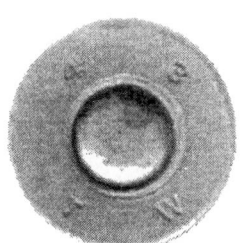

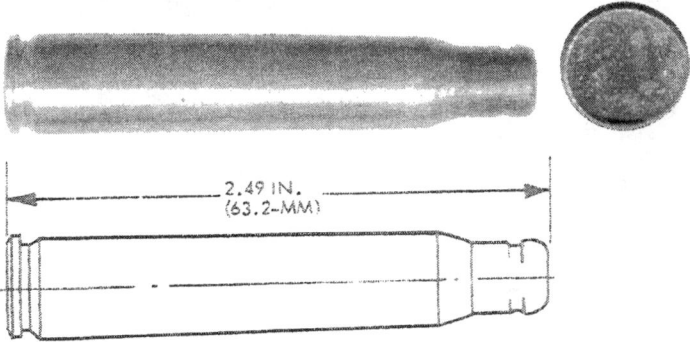

SPECIMEN DIMENSIONS

Rim Measurement: .470
Neck Measurement: .335
Bullet Diameter: N /A
Case Length: 2.49

OTHER DETAILS

Caliber: .30 Springfield
Manufacture Date: 1943
Specialty: Blank M1909
Cartridge Type: Rifle / Mg

Blank Cartridge

General Information: This U.S. Springfield model 1909 blank cartridge which enclosed 12 grains of powder with a red paper disc was primarily used for training purposes and ceremonies. The date of manufacture pictured on the headstamp may not normally be accurate due to the practice of reusing cases for blank production, however this specimen came from an apparently new and unopened box wherein all rounds were so dated.

UNITED STATES

Arsenal: Kings Mills Ordnance Plant
Kings Mills, Ohio (Peters Cartridge Co.)

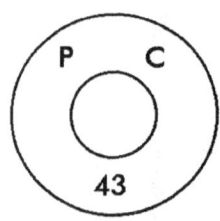

Headstamp

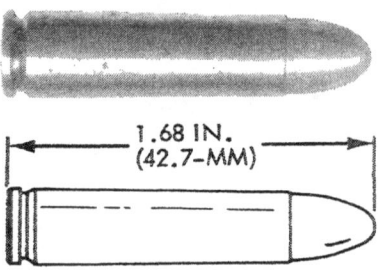

Side View

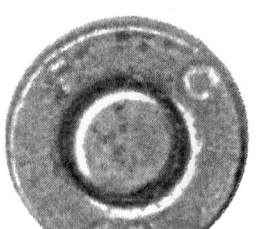

SPECIMEN DIMENSIONS

Rim Measurement: .356
Neck Measurement: .330
Bullet Diameter: .305
Case Length: 1.280

.30 M1 Carbine

OTHER DETAILS

Caliber: .30 M1
Manufacture Date: 1943
Specialty: Ball
Cartridge Type: Carbine

General Information: The Kings Mills ordnance plant was one of the largest volume producers of .30 caliber carbine ammunition. The .30 M1 Carbine was mostly used in the pacific theater, however some quantity was issued for the Normandy invasion. The creation of this cartridge had a significant impact on the Pacific Theater of operations during WW II due to the small maneuverable size of the carbine in the jungle environment. Although many people would argue about the lack of stopping power this cartridge has to offer. Its original purpose was to augment the scarcity of the .45 Pistol and serve as a "behind the front, supply line" weapon.

UNITED STATES

Arsenal: Lake City Ordnance Plant
Independence, Missouri

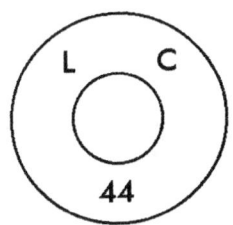

Headstamp

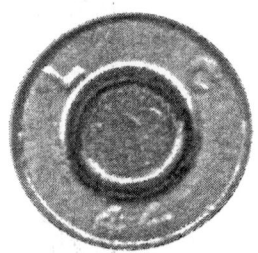

Side View

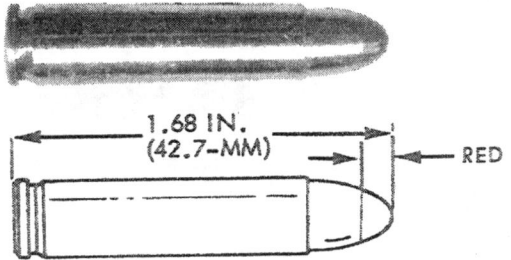

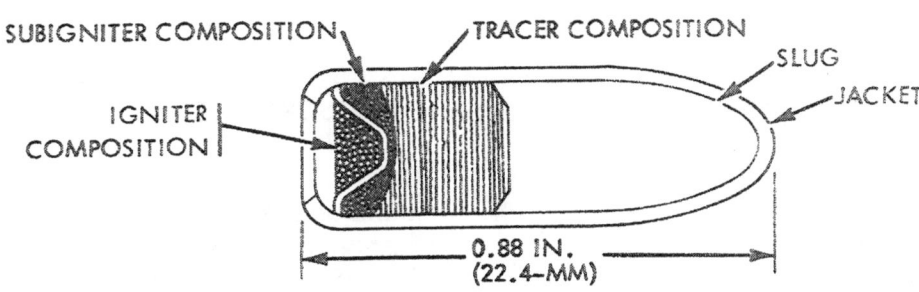

SPECIMEN DIMENSIONS

Rim Measurement: .356
Neck Measurement: .330
Bullet Diameter: .305
Case Length: 1.280

.30 M1 Carbine Tracer

OTHER DETAILS

Caliber: .30
Manufacture Date: 1944
Specialty: Tracer, Red
Cartridge Type: Carbine

Overall Length: 1.68

General Information: This is the tracer round for the M1 carbine which would display a trace of full luminosity after no more then 100 yards lasting up to 400 yards. Although this round is easily identified by its red tip, carbine tracers can also be found with an orange tip signifying day tracer use. Like the ball round, a pressure of 40,000 psi is exerted when the cartridge is fired.

UNITED STATES

Arsenal: Lake City Ordnance Plant
Independence, Missouri

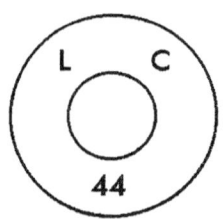

Headstamp

Side View

SPECIMEN DIMENSIONS

Rim Measurement: .356
Neck Measurement: .330
Bullet Diameter: N/a
Case Length: 1.286

OTHER DETAILS

Caliber: .30 M1
Manufacture Date: 1944
Specialty: Grenade
Cartridge Type: Carbine

M1 Carbine grenade round used during World War II

General Information: This round is not to be confused with a blank cartridge, the M6 grenade blank functions as an ignition source for rifle grenades of the period and is very specialized. The specimen shown above came from Lake City boxed Lot 12098, was in remarkable condition for its age. Boxes certainly can make a difference in preserving cartridges as long as they are kept in a dry location.

I find it amusing that some collector's will only buy a cartridge after it has turned brown from oxidation because they say " it looks it's age". When you remove a cartridge from its original sealed box it can look as new as the day it was made or issued to the troops. How can you get more original then that? However, I suppose it would make a good sales pitch to sell your old brown stuff. So don't worry, the shiny ones turn brown too if you wait a few years.

UNITED STATES

Arsenal: Lake City Ordnance Plant
Independence, Missouri

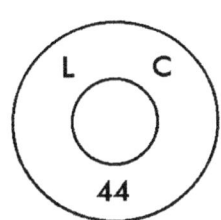

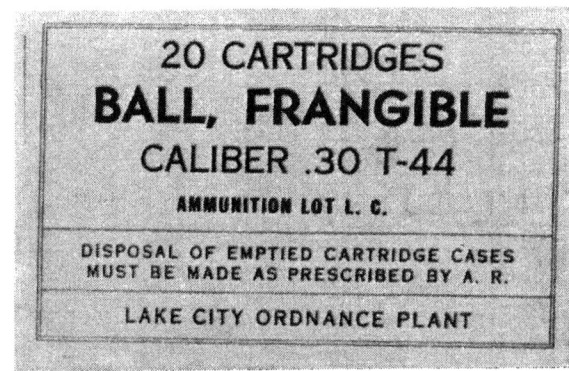

Headstamp

Side View

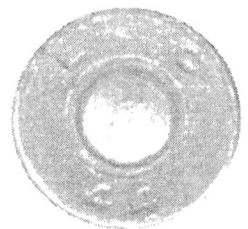

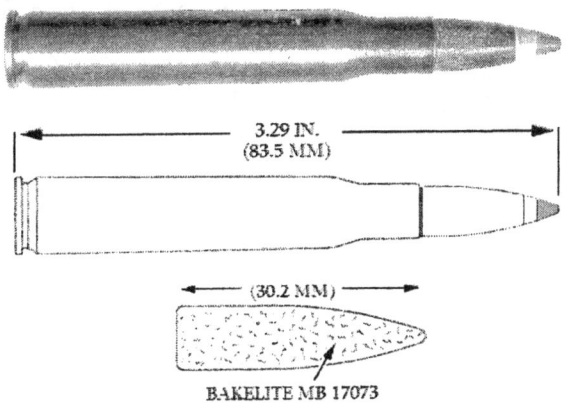

SPECIMEN DIMENSIONS

Rim Measurement: .468
Neck Measurement: .332
Bullet Diameter: .308
Case Length: 2.478

OTHER DETAILS

Caliber: .30
Manufacture Date: 1944
Specialty: Frangible
Cartridge Type: MG

.30 T-44 Frangible Practice round

General Information: Mainly developed for firing at targets pulled by airplanes. The bullet was comprised of a Bakelite-bonded lead powder so it could not penetrate or damage the essential systems of the tow plane. Bullet tips are painted green over white field. Notice the double label on this box, what could be underneath? A duplicate label was found.

UNITED STATES

Arsenal: Frankford
Philadelphia, Pennsylvania

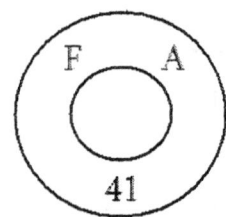

Headstamp

Side View

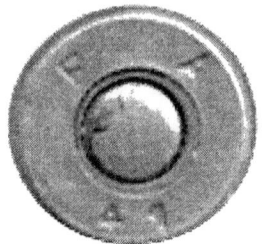

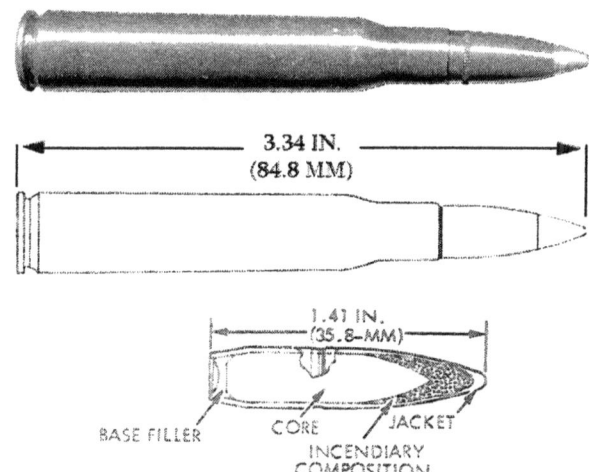

DIMENSIONS

Rim Measurement: .468
Neck Measurement: .335
Bullet Diameter: .308
Case Length: 2.480

.30 Incendiary

OTHER DETAILS

Caliber: .30
Manufacture Date: 1941
Specialty: Incendiary
Cartridge Type: Rifle / Mg

General Information: Originally created to set wooden structures and Zeppelins on fire during the First World War. The incendiary cartridge would lead manufacturers to other special purpose uses, such as spotting rounds and smoke cartridges.

UNITED STATES

Arsenal: Winchester Repeating Arms
New Haven, Connecticut

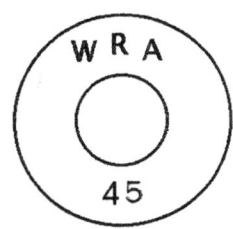

Headstamp

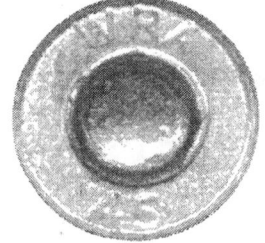

Side View

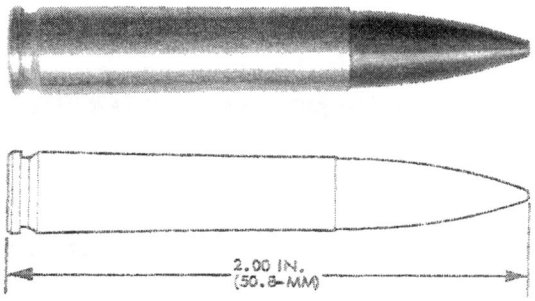

SPECIMEN DIMENSIONS

Rim Measurement: .356
Neck Measurement: .330
Bullet Diameter: .307
Case Length: 1.285

OTHER DETAILS

Caliber: .30
Manufacture Date: 1945
Specialty: Proof
Cartridge Type: Carbine

.30 M1 High pressure chamber test cartridge

General information: Firing this cartridge exerted approximately 50,000 pounds of pressure per square inch on the carbines chamber for testing purposes. The above cartridge has a tinned case for identification as a proof round. The primer cup also appears to be tinned.

TURKEY

Arsenal: **TCFS (Turkiye Cumhuriyeti) Fabrikalar Iskenderun, Iskenderun (Skenderun)**

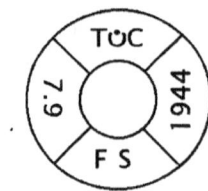

Headstamp

Side View

SPECIMEN DIMENSIONS

Rim Measurement: .465
Neck Measurement: .353
Bullet diameter: .322
Case Length: 2.241

7.92x57 Ball

OTHER DETAILS

Caliber: 7.92x57
Manufacture Date: 1944
Specialty: Ball
Cartridge type: Rifle / Mg

Overall Length: 3.170

General Information This cartridge was made during WWII when Turkey was an ally of Germany. The city of Iskenderun, pronounced Skenderun by its current inhabitants, was originally named Alexandretta after Alexander the Great. During the crusades, this city was an important arrival point in the region due to its deep-water port. This ball cartridge has a black primer annulus.

SWITZERLAND

Arsenal: Solothurn

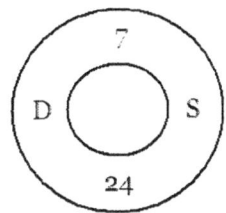

Headstamp

Side View

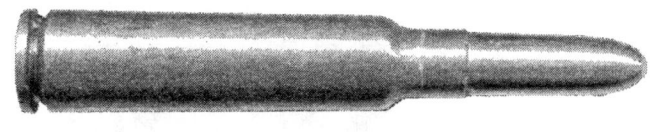

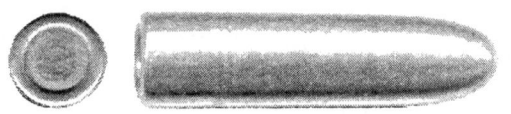

SPECIMEN DIMENSIONS

Rim Measurement: .496
Neck Measurement: .335
Bullet diameter: .306
Case Length: 2.145

OTHER DETAILS

Caliber: 7.5x55
Manufacture Date: 1924
Specialty: Ball
Cartridge type: Rifle

Overall Length: 3.51

General Information This round nosed cartridge specimen was made for the model 90/03 Schmidt-Rubin rifle, it has a steel capped hollow based lead bullet followed by a 190 grain iron-jacket.

SOVIET UNION
RUSSIA - USSR - CCCP

Arsenal: Russian Government Arsenal 60,
Frunze, Kirgisia,

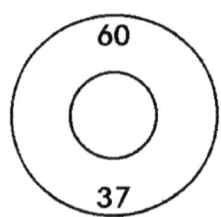

Headstamp

Side View

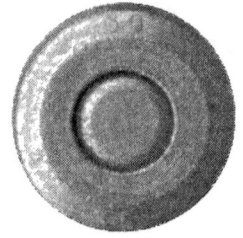
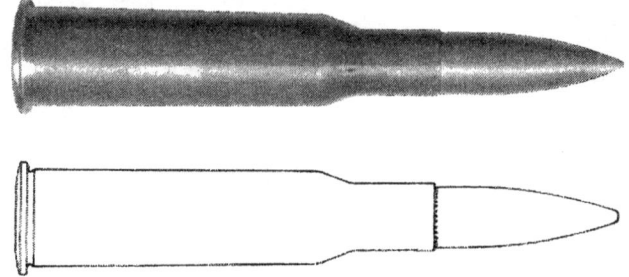

SPECIMEN DIMENSIONS

Rim Measurement: .568
Neck Measurement: .332
Bullet Diameter: .310
Case Length: 2.110

7.62 Heavy Ball

OTHER DETAILS

Caliber: 7.62 x 54R
Manufacture Date: 1937
Specialty: Heavy Ball
Cartridge Type: Rifle / MG

General Information: This Russian 7.62x54 rimmed cartridge made for the Mosin-Nagant system rifle or carbine reached a muzzle velocity of 2800 f.p.s. The yellow tip denotes the color code for heavy ball as specified in the color code table on page 27 of this guide.

JAPAN

Arsenal: Imperial Japanese Army, Tokyo

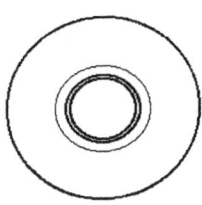

Headstamp

Side View

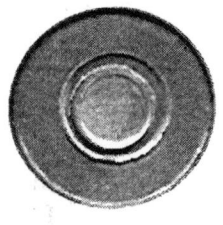
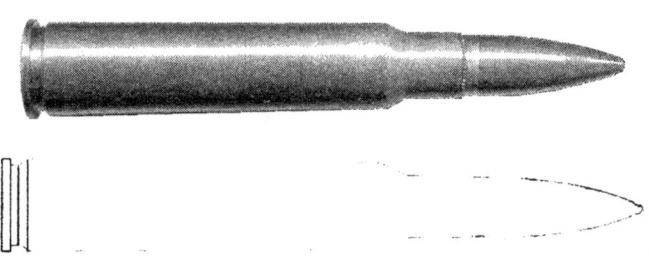

SPECIMEN DIMENSIONS

Rim Measurement: .496
Neck Measurement: .336
Bullet Diameter: .310
Case Length: 2.270

7.7 Semi Rimmed Ball

OTHER DETAILS

Caliber: 7.7 x 58SR
Manufacture Date: WWII
Specialty: Ball
Cartridge Type: Rifle / MG

Overall Length: 3.143

General Information: This cartridge is semi rimmed, which means the rim, protrudes above the level of the case sidewall about half the distance a rimmed version would. The pink case mouth band easily identifies the ball round. The lack of a headstamp denotes that the round was manufactured for the army as only navy contracts allowed a headstamp marking. The muzzle velocity reached 2300 f.p.s.

JAPAN

Arsenal: Imperial Japanese Army
Tokyo

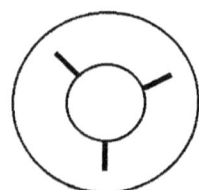

LATE TYPE - 139 Grain Bullet

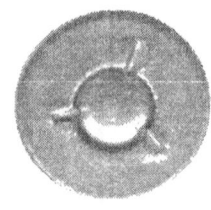

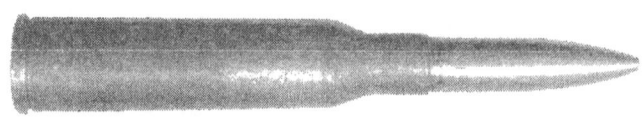

Headstamp   Side View

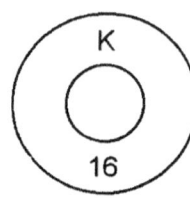

EARLY TYPE - 163 Grain Bullet

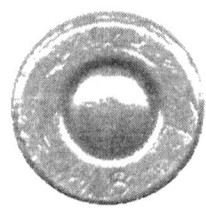

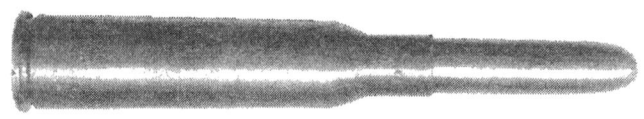

SPECIMEN DIMENSIONS

Rim Measurement: .476
Neck Measurement: .290
Bullet Diameter: .262
Case Length: 1.998

Arisaka Semi Rimmed Ball

OTHER DETAILS

Caliber: 6.5mm
Manufacture Date: N/a
Specialty: Ball
Cartridge Type: Rifle

Overall Length: 2.990

General Information: The late type ball round is identified by the pink band around the bullet near the case mouth. The muzzle velocity of the late type round reached 2,500 f.p.s. and the early type loading reached 2,390 f.p.s. made by Kynoch for a large 1916 Japanese contract.

JAPAN

Arsenal: Imperial Japanese Army
Tokyo

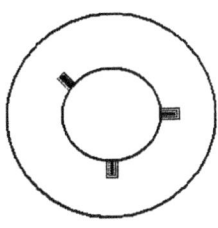

Headstamp

Side View

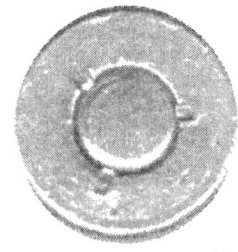

SPECIMEN DIMENSIONS

Rim Measurement: .468
Neck Measurement: .350
Bullet diameter: .320
Case Length: 2.238

HIGH EXPLOSIVE (Petn)

OTHER DETAILS

Caliber: 7.92 x 57
Manufacture Date: 1940s
Specialty: HE
Cartridge type: Rifle

Overall Length: 3.164

General information: This flat nosed bullet has a special purpose, to detonate a powerful high explosive charge contained inside upon impact with its target. One of the more scarier rounds to handle, the explosive (Petn) compound is unstable enough that it may go off if you drop it to the floor or otherwise fail to show the proper respect. This cartridge can also be identified by the white case mouth seal.

ITALY

Arsenal: Societa Metallurgica Italiana
Campo Tizzore

Headstamp

Side View

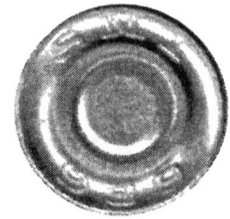

SPECIMEN DIMENSIONS

Rim Measurement: .446
Neck Measurement: .325
Bullet Diameter: .298
Case Length: 2.008

7.35 Carcano

OTHER DETAILS

Caliber: 7.35 x 51
Manufacture Date:: 1939
Specialty: Ball
Cartridge Type: Rifle

General information: "Cartucce a pallottola per armi mod 38", was the official designation for this cartridge. Translated, it was produced for the bolt action Carcano Model 1938 rifle & carbine replacing the smaller and ineffective 6.5 MM cartridge used during the Ethiopian campaign. The projectile is comprised of 50% aluminum and 50% lead core within a copper metal jacket. The Muzzle velocity of this cartridge reached 2400 f.p.s.

ITALY

Arsenal: Pirotechnia da Bologna
Bologna

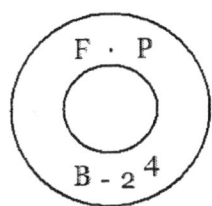

Headstamp

Side View

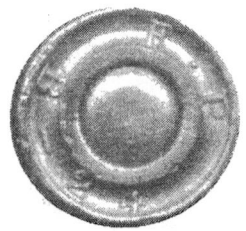

SPECIMEN DIMENSIONS

Rim Measurement: .442
Neck Measurement: .292
Bullet Diameter: .262
Case Length: 2.053

6.5 Model 1891 Carcano

OTHER DETAILS

Caliber: 6.5 x 52.5mm
Manufacture Date: 1924
Specialty: **Multi-ball**
Cartridge Type: **Rifle**

General Information: This multi-ball cartridge or "cartuccia a mitraglia" has an extraordinarily long projectile (about 2 inches). The jacket has 3 slits, which run longitudinally up the long access with a jacketed ball at the tip. These slits allow the projectiles to be thrown as a volley or shot pattern when fired. Possibly for use as a guard cartridge.

ITALY

Arsenal: Societa Metallurgica Italiana
          Campo Tizzore

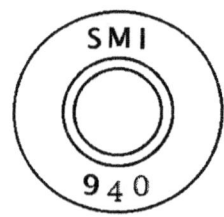

Headstamp

Side View

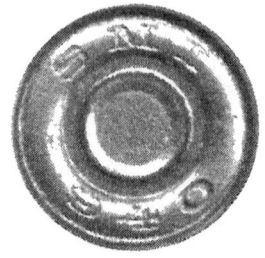

SPECIMEN DIMENSIONS

Rim Measurement: .470
Neck Measurement: .359
Bullet Diameter: .328
Case Length: 2.319

8mm Breda Machine Gun

OTHER DETAILS

Caliber: 8 x 59 mm
Manufacture Date: 1940
Specialty: Ball
Cartridge Type: Mg

Overall Length: 3.167

General Information: This cartridge is the ball loading for the Italian Breda Model 37/38 machine gun. A very effective machine gun round developed with the guidance of the German Wehrmacht during World War II. Both brass and steel cases have been noted as well as Armor Piercing, AP Tracer and observation / spotting rounds examined.

ITALY

Arsenal: Pirotechnia di Capua, Capua

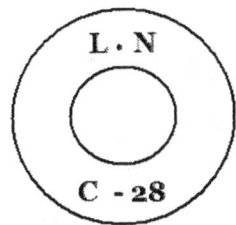

Headstamp

Side View

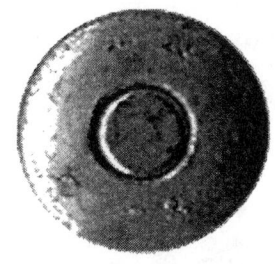
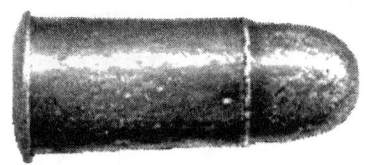

SPECIMEN DIMENSIONS

Rim Measurement: .505
Neck Measurement: .444
Bullet diameter: .422
Case Length: .890

10.4mm Revolver

OTHER DETAILS

Caliber: 10.4mm
Manufacture Date: 1928
Specialty: Ball
Cartridge type: Revolver

Overall Length: 1.25

General Information The bullet of this cartridge seats flush with the case mouth by flanging outward to meet it. The projectile is further secured by three stab crimps on the neck of the case. The bullet appears to be bronze and the primer cup is copper. The letters L.N on the top rim are the chief government inspectors initials.

ISRAEL

Arsenal: Arab Manufacture, Captured…

Headstamp

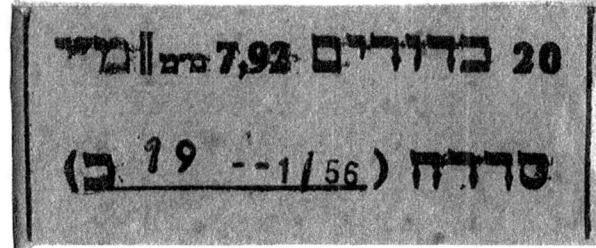

Side View

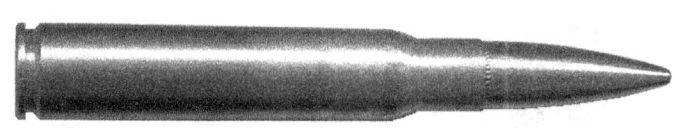

SPECIMEN DIMENSIONS

Rim Measurement: .466
Neck Measurement: .349
Bullet diameter: .322
Case Length: 2.232

7.92x57 Ball

OTHER DETAILS

Caliber: 7.92x57
Manufacture Date: 1956
Specialty: **Ball**
Cartridge type: **Rifle**

Overall Length: 3.162

General Information During and after the war for Israeli Independence there was a great need for small arms. A large number of Mauser rifles were cheaply available from various sources, which were purchased and pressed into service. Some munitions were purchased or captured from various Arab sources. The following color code system was used to identify specialty or function, but it was only valid for 7.92x57 cartridges.

Bullet tip color	Primer annulus color	Function type
None	Purple	Ball
Red	Green	Tracer
Black	Green	AP
Black	Red	API
Blue	Green	Incendiary

GERMANY

Arsenal: "aux" Polte
Madgeburg

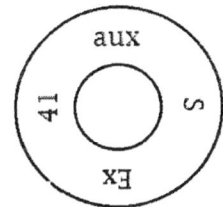

Headstamp

Side View

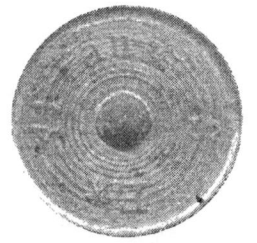

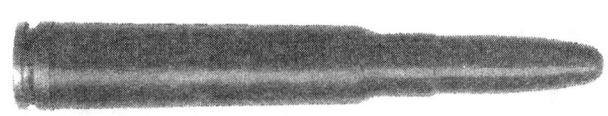

SPECIMEN DIMENSIONS

Rim Measurement: .467
Neck Measurement: .340
Bullet Diameter: .310
Case Length: 2.218

OTHER DETAILS

Caliber: 7.92 x 57
Manufacture Date: 1941
Specialty: Plastic Exercise
Cartridge Type: Rifle / MG

Exercise round – No Powder – No Primer

General Information: The Ex on the headstamp indicates that this is an exercise or (Exerzier) cartridge used for dry firing to detect and correct flinching. Comprised of a steel plug on the end of the remaining one-piece plastic body, which weighs a little less then an actual cartridge. Black plastic specimens are little harder to find then the red, however both types are scarce especially those manufactured by Polte.

GERMANY

Arsenal: "aux" Polte Madgeburg Works
Madgeburg

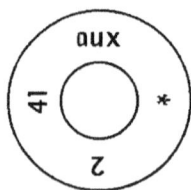

Headstamp					Side View

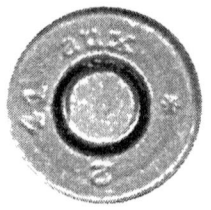

SPECIMEN DIMENSIONS

Rim Measurement: .390
Neck Measurement: 379
Bullet Diameter: .353
Case Length: .752

9mm Luger P-08 / P-38

OTHER DETAILS

Caliber: 9x19mm
Manufacture Date: 1941
Specialty: Heavy Ball
Cartridge Type: Pistol

Overall Length: 1.16

General Information: The box pictured above is marked m.E. (mit Eisenkern) (mild steel core) or heavy ball. Was this an attempt to augment the 9mm cartridge with some additional stopping power?

GERMANY

Arsenal: Deutsche Metallpatronenfabrik, Karlsruhe

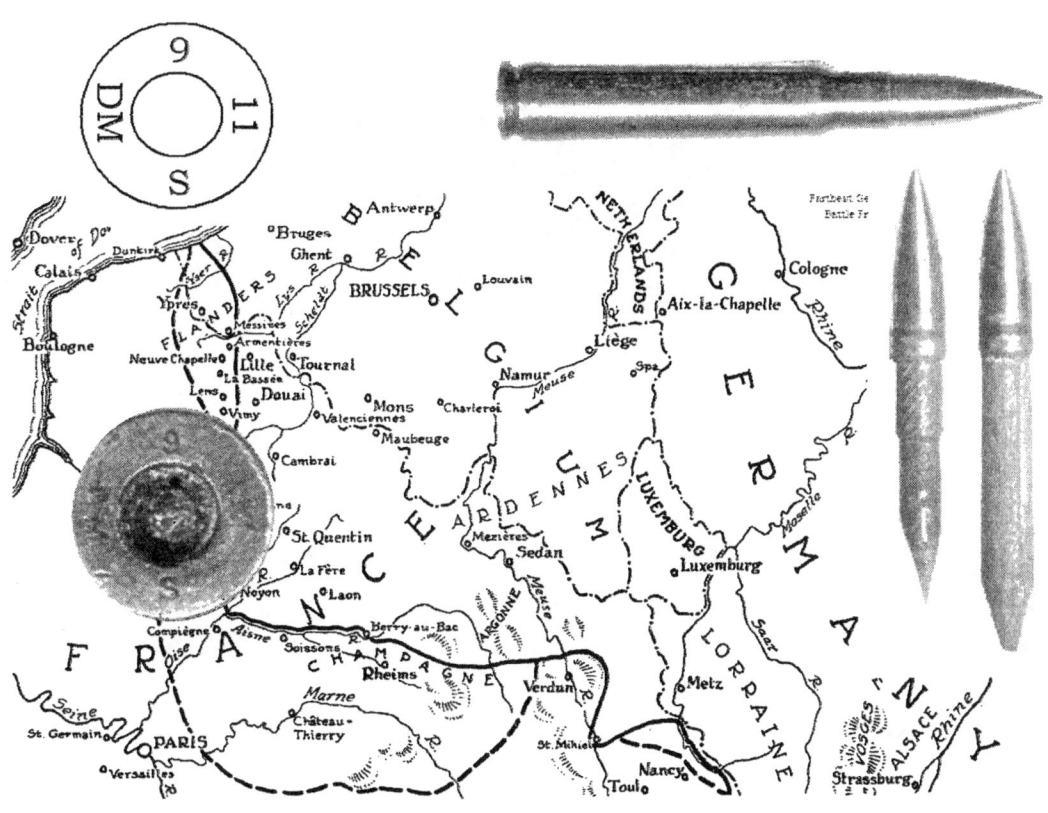

SPECIMEN DIMENSIONS

Rim Measurement: .460
Neck Measurement: .350
Bullet Diameter: .320
Case Length: 2.235

Pen / Pencil cartridges - World War I

OTHER DETAILS

Caliber: 7.92 x 57
Manufacture Date: 1911 & 1913
Specialty: Writing
Cartridge Type: N/A

Overall Length: 3.125

General Information: These unusual cartridge modifications make these disguised writing implements inconspicuous yet handy for writing letters to home or perhaps some important communications in the trenches. One can imagine an officer writing down orders for subordinates or perhaps calling for an artillery barrage minutes before that final charge. But whatever the circumstances, they will certainly help us to see the human face behind the grim aspect of war. Ordinary people placed in extraordinary circumstances by the leaders of their respective nations.

Arsenal: Polte, Madgeburg

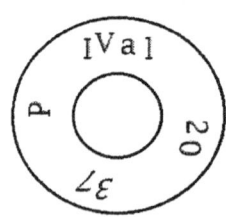

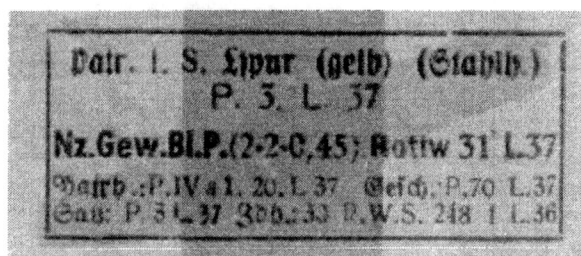

Headstamp

Side View

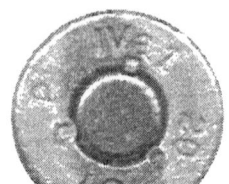

SPECIMEN DIMENSIONS

Rim Measurement: .468
Neck Measurement: .350
Bullet Diameter: .320
Case Length: 2.238

Standard type round used during World War II

OTHER DETAILS

Caliber: 7.92 x 57
Manufacture Date: 1937
Specialty: Practice tracer
Cartridge Type: MG

Overall Length: 3.164

General Information: This practice tracer cartridge was produced for the Luftwaffe, the jacketed aluminum core surrounds a tube containing the (gelb) yellow tracing compound. Identification is by the green stripe across the base and black tip. The muzzle velocity of this cartridge reached 3,020 f.p.s.

GERMANY

Arsenal: Polte
Madgeburg

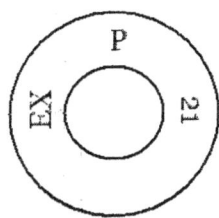

Headstamp

Side View

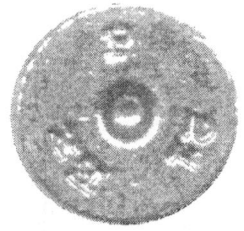
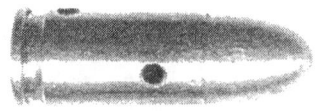

SPECIMEN DIMENSIONS

Rim Measurement: .391
Neck Measurement: .377
Bullet Diameter: .352
Case Length: 747

OTHER DETAILS

Caliber: 9mm
Manufacture Date: 1921
Specialty: Exercise
Cartridge Type: Luger

Exercise round - No Powder – No Primer

General Information: The Ex on the headstamp indicates that this is an exercise round. This tinned lightweight holed dummy was used for practice drilling which allowed the safe dry firing of the 9mm parabellum or P08. Several variations can be found having no holes or bullet cores but most are either tinned or chrome plated.

GERMANY

Arsenal: P-334 Mansfield
Rothenberg-Saale

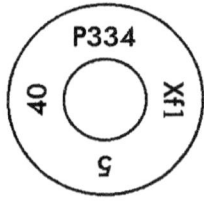

Headstamp

Side View

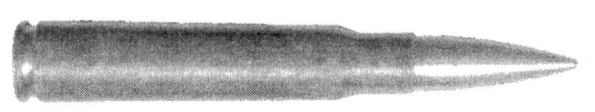

SPECIMEN DIMENSIONS

Rim Measurement: .470
Neck Measurement: .350
Bullet Diameter: .322
Case Length: 2.240

Heavy Ball

OTHER DETAILS

Caliber: 7.92 x 57
Manufacture Date: 1940
Specialty: Heavy Ball (s.S.)
Cartridge Type: Rifle / MG

Overall Length: 3.162

General Information: The bullet of this cartridge has a hard lead core and an ingot steel jacket plated with tombac, making it (schweres Spitzengeschoss) or heavy ball. The entire cartridge case of this specimen is coated with a greenish lacquer. The muzzle velocity of this cartridge reached 2,428 f.p.s.

GERMANY

Arsenal: "hla" Metallwarenfabrik – Treuenbrietzen, Gmbh
Sebandushof

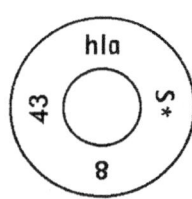

Headstamp

Side View

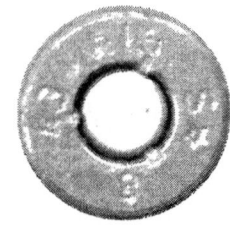

SPECIMEN DIMENSIONS

Rim Measurement: .465
Neck Measurement: .350
Bullet Diameter: .320
Case Length: 2.238

Semi Armor Piercing

OTHER DETAILS

Caliber: 7.92 x 57
Manufacture Date: 1943
Specialty: SmE
Cartridge Type: MG / Rifle

Overall Length: 3.160

General Information: S.m.E. (Spitzen mit Eisenkern) is a semi-armor piercing round with a soft iron or mild steel core surrounded by lead and a standard jacket. Identifiable by the blue primer annulus. Notice the three primer stab crimps. This cartridge reached a muzzle velocity of 2,860 f.p.s. This round was preferred for the machine gun "fur MG" but was also used in rifles.

GERMANY

Arsenal: "P-635" Gustloff-Werke, Otto Eberhardt Patronenfabrik
Hirtenberg, Austria

Headstamp

Side View

SPECIMEN DIMENSIONS

Rim Measurement: .554
Neck Measurement: .360
Bullet diameter: .326
Case Length: 2.185

Solothurn Machine Gun Ball

OTHER DETAILS

Caliber: 8x56Rmm
Manufacture Date: 1938
Specialty: Ball
Cartridge type: MG

Overall Length: 3.07

General information: This cartridge was solely produced for use in the Solothurn Machine Gun developed in 1930. One of the few cartridges actually stamped with the new symbol of the Reich, the eagle and swastika. This rimmed cartridge with its overall husky appearance distinguishes it from all other 8-mm cartridges.

GERMANY

Arsenal: P-315 Markisches Walzwerke, Stausberg, Bez- Potsdam

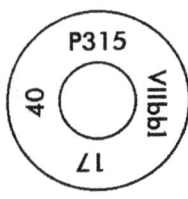

Headstamp

Side View

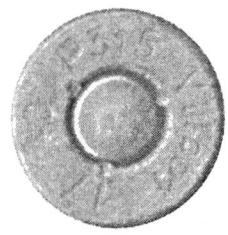

SPECIMEN DIMENSIONS

Rim Measurement: .466
Neck Measurement: .348
Bullet Diameter: .322
Case Length: 2.240

Semi – Armor Piercing

OTHER DETAILS

Caliber: 7.92 x 57
Manufacture Date: 1940
Specialty: Ball
Cartridge Type: Rifle / Mg

Overall Length: 3.160

General Information: S.M.E. (Spitzen mit Eisenkern) is a semi-armor piercing round with a soft iron or mild steel core surrounded by lead and a standard jacket. Identifiable by the blue primer annulus. Notice the three primer stab crimps. This cartridge reached a muzzle velocity of 2860 f.p.s.

GERMANY

Arsenal: "P-69" Patronen-Zundhutchen und Metallwarenfabrik, Shoenbeck

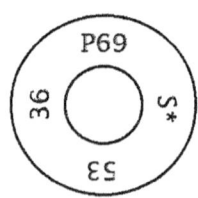

Headstamp

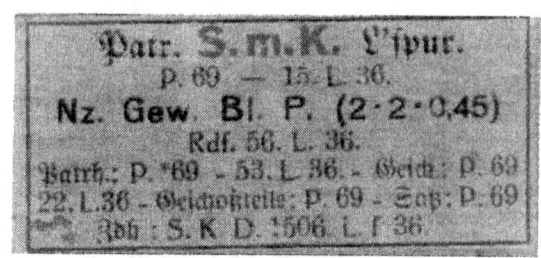

Side View

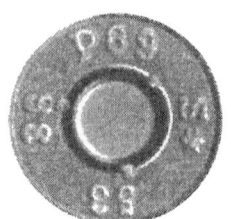

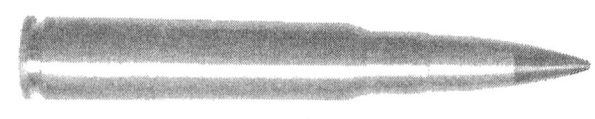

SPECIMEN DIMENSIONS

Rim Measurement: .466
Neck Measurement: .348
Bullet Diameter: .322
Case Length: 2.235

Armor Piercing Tracer

OTHER DETAILS

Caliber: 7.92 x 57
Manufacture Date: 1936
Specialty: A. P. Tracer
Cartridge Type: Rifle / Mg

Overall Length: 3.160

General Information: S. m. K. (Spitzen mit Kern) is an armor piercing round with a (L'spur) or "Leutch spur" tracer compound leaving a trajectory of red, green or yellow. The elements responsible for these colors are magnesium powder and barium nitrate. The red primer annulus and black bullet tip easily identifies this cartridge. Notice the primer stab crimps.

GERMANY

Arsenal: "hla" Metallwarenfabrik – Treuenbrietzen, Gmbh
Sebandushof

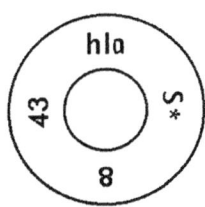

Headstamp

Side View

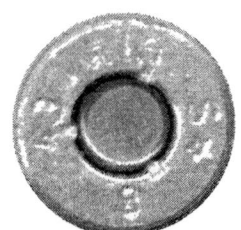

SPECIMEN DIMENSIONS

Rim Measurement: .470
Neck Measurement: .350
Bullet Diameter: .323
Case Length: 2.238

Armor Piercing

OTHER DETAILS

Caliber: 7.92 x 57
Manufacture Date: 1943
Specialty: A P
Cartridge Type: Rifle / MG

Overall Length: 3.162

General Information: The S.m.K. or (Spitzengechoss mit Kern) armor piercing (S bullet with a hardened core) has a core of steel with a lead envelope further enclosed with the standard jacket. Identifiable by a red primer annulus (notice the primer stab crimps). This specimen also has a green halo or ring around the bullet at mid point indicating a tropic pack weather seal. The -v mark on the box label indicates an improved velocity load. The S star marking on the headstamp denotes a steel case.

FRANCE

Arsenal: Cartoucherie du Mans,
Le Mans

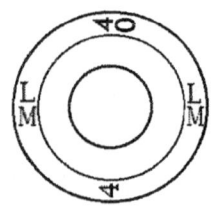

Headstamp

Side View

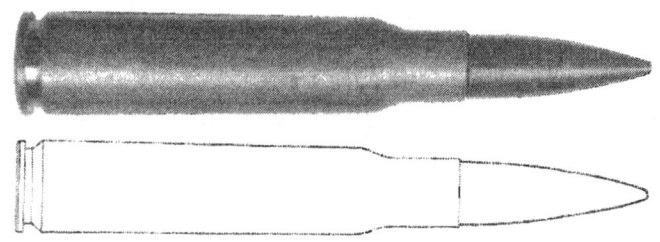

SPECIMEN DIMENSIONS

Rim Measurement: .486
Neck Measurement: .341
Bullet diameter: .304
Case Length: 2.112

1936 MAS Rifle Heavy ball

OTHER DETAILS

Caliber: 7.5 x 54
Manufacture Date: 1940
Specialty: Heavy Ball M 1929D
Cartridge type: Rifle

General information: This cartridge is the same as the Ball or "balle" C except for the heavier (longer) projectile which has a "boat tailed" base. The round can be easily identified by its blackened bullet. The muzzle velocity of this cartridge reached 2200 f.p.s.

FRANCE

Arsenal: Atelier de Construction de Rennes
Rennes,

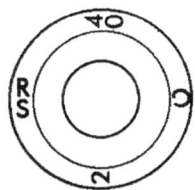

Headstamp

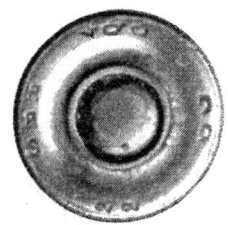

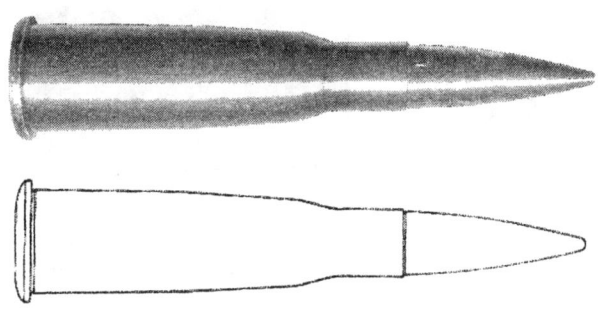

Side View

SPECIMEN DIMENSIONS

Rim Measurement: .626
Neck Measurement: .348
Bullet diameter: .324
Case Length: 1.962

OTHER DETAILS

Caliber: 8 x 50R
Manufacture Date: 1940
Specialty: Ball D
Cartridge type: Rifle

Standard type round used during both World Wars

General information: This cartridge was produced for the Model 1886 Lebel bolt action rifle. A protective groove encircles the primer and this specimen's headstamp has been double struck. The earlier versions were the first cartridge used in military rifles of a major power with a pointed bronze projectile and smokeless powder. The muzzle velocity of this cartridge reached 2380 f.p.s.

FRANCE

Arsenal: Societe Francaise des Munitions
Paris,

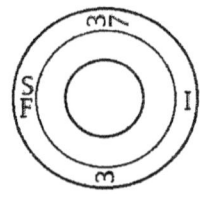

Headstamp

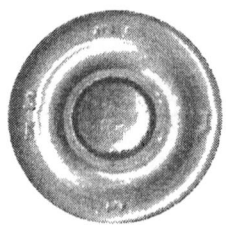

Side View

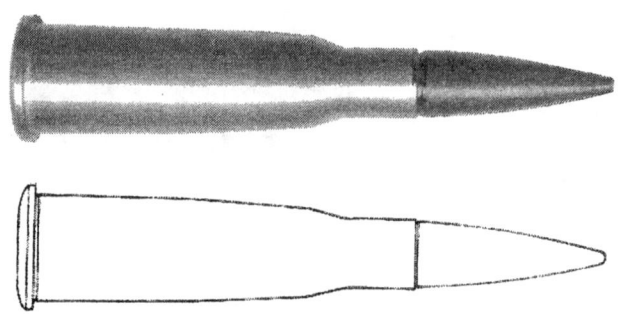

SPECIMEN DIMENSIONS

Rim Measurement: .630
Neck Measurement: .350
Bullet Diameter: .324
Case Length: 1.978

OTHER DETAILS

Caliber: 8 x 50R
Manufacture Date: 1937
Specialty: Armor Piercing
Cartridge Type: Rifle / MG

Standard type round used during both World Wars

General Information: This blackened flat-based bullet identifies this cartridge as an armor piercing or "perforante" round originally produced for machine guns but popularly used by the troops in their rifles. A groove encircles and protects the primer.

FRANCE

Arsenal: Atelier de Construction de Tarbles
Tarbles,

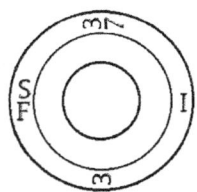

Headstamp

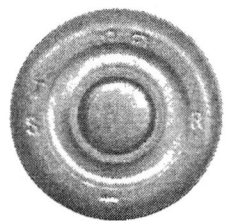

Side View

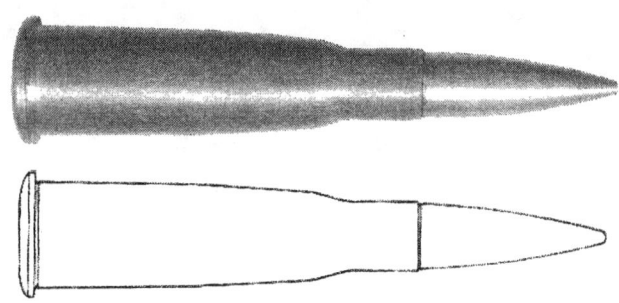

SPECIMEN DIMENSIONS

Rim Measurement: .628
Neck Measurement: .350
Bullet Diameter: .328
Case Length: 1.982

OTHER DETAILS

Caliber: 8 x 50R
Manufacture Date: 1939
Specialty: Tracer
Cartridge Type: Rifle / MG

Standard type tracer round used during World War II

General Information: The tin washed wedge-based bullet identifies this tracer loading of the standard ball round. This cartridge was originally produced for machine guns but it was also used in rifles. As usual a groove encircles the primer. Notice the R on the opposite side of the rim from the manufacturers code, it identifies the company that supplied the raw metal for the case.

FRANCE

Arsenal: Atelier de Construction ? (Variation)

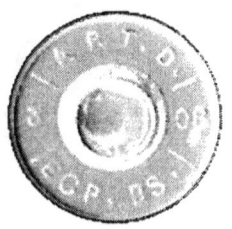

Headstamp

Side View

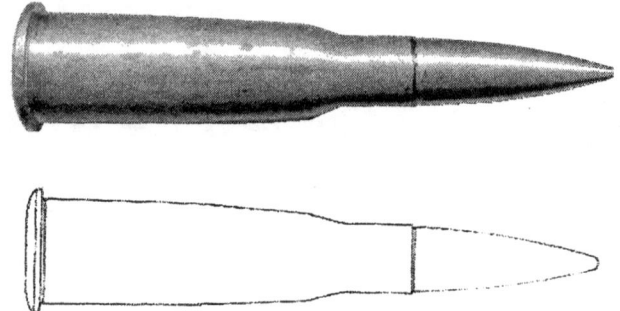

SPECIMEN DIMENSIONS

Rim Measurement: .629
Neck Measurement: .348
Bullet Diameter: .325
Case Length: 1.965

8 mm Lebel Rifle

OTHER DETAILS

Caliber: 8 x 50 R
Manufacture Date: 1908
Specialty: Ball
Cartridge Type: Rifle / Mg

Overall Length: 2.949

General Information: This cartridge was a bit of a surprise in that I had not previously encountered this headstamp before now. The ECP. BS. are the metal supplier's for the bullet and case materials.

FRANCE

Arsenal: Parc d' Artillerie de Place de Verdun
Verdun

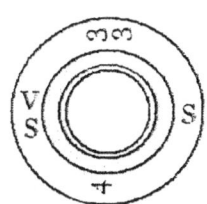

Headstamp

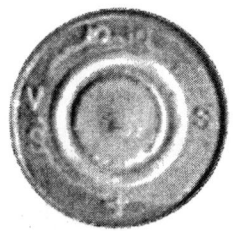

Side View

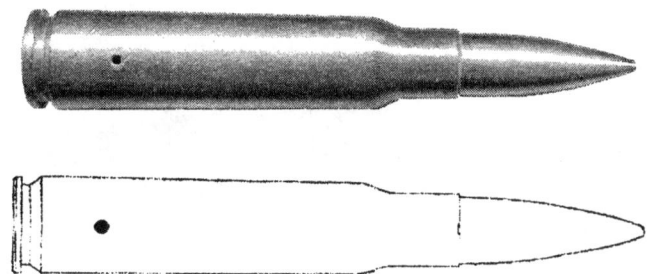

SPECIMEN DIMENSIONS

Rim Measurement: .486
Neck Measurement: .341
Bullet Diameter: .304
Case Length: 2.115

1936 MAS Rifle

OTHER DETAILS

Caliber: 7.5 x 54
Manufacture Date: 1933
Specialty: Exercise Dummy
Cartridge Type: Rifle

Overall Length: 3.91

General Information: This cartridge was used to practice dry firing in order to detect flinching. You may notice some of the wash on the case is starting wear off. The false primer has been struck numerous times indicating this round has been used. There is a small hole in the side of the case .510 inches from the rim to help distinguish it from live rounds.

FRANCE

Arsenal: Parc d' Artillerie de Place de Verdun
Verdun

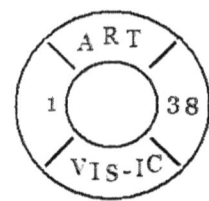

Headstamp   Side View

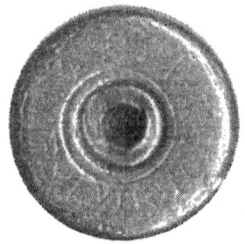 

SPECIMEN DIMENSIONS

Rim Measurement: .628
Neck Measurement: .350
Bullet diameter: .318
Case Length: 1.982

OTHER DETAILS

Caliber: 8 x 50R
Manufacture Date: 1938
Specialty: Dummy
Cartridge type: Rifle

Dummy "exercise" round World War II

General information: This dummy practice round is somewhat unusual among cartridges of its type in that it has a brass base and a brass front in place of the projectile with wood in between. The other letters on the headstamp denotes the company supplying the raw materials used for the production of the cartridge. The primary purpose of this type of cartridge is to detect flinching while dry firing the rifle, which protects the firing pin from damage.

FINLAND

Arsenal: Valition Patruunatehdas
         Lapua

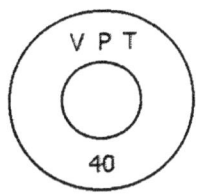

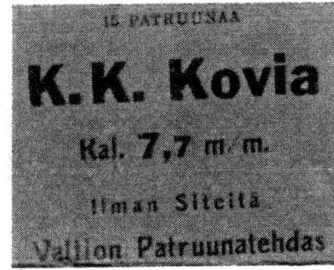

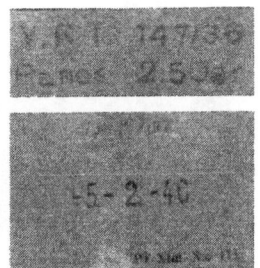

Headstamp

Side View

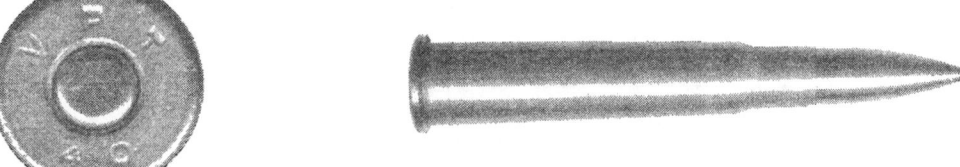

SPECIMEN DIMENSIONS

Rim Measurement: 533
Neck Measurement: 337
Bullet Diameter: 311
Case Length: 2.282

OTHER DETAILS

Caliber: 7.7 / .303
Manufacture Date: 1940
Specialty: Ball
Cartridge Type: Rifle / MG

Standard type round used during World War II

General Information: Made in Finland by Valition Patruunatehdas of Lapua these rimmed ball cartridges have brass primers.

FINLAND

Arsenal: Russian Government Arsenal 60,
Frunze, Kirgisia, Russia

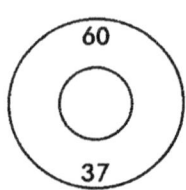

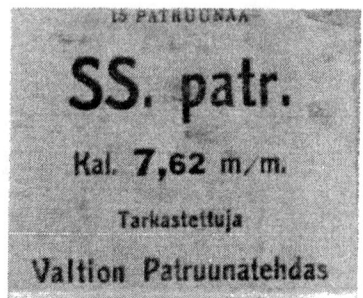

Headstamp

Side View

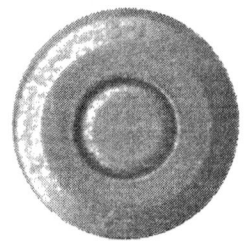

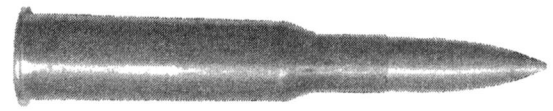

SPECIMEN DIMENSIONS

Rim Measurement: .566
Neck Measurement: .332
Bullet Diameter: .310
Case Length: 2.100

OTHER DETAILS

Caliber: 7.62 x 54R
Manufacture Date: 1937-41
Specialty: Ball
Cartridge Type: Rifle / MG

Standard type round used during World War II

General Information: This box bearing a Finish label (15 cartridges of 7.62 m/m) is actually a captured box of Russian 7.62x54R Mosin-Nagant ball cartridges bearing dates ranging from 1937 to 1941. Acquired for use in the many captured Russian rifles and carbines.

INDIA
(BRITISH RULE)

Arsenal: Kirkee Arsenal
Kirkee

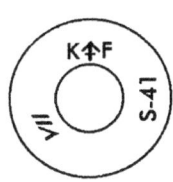

Headstamp

Side View

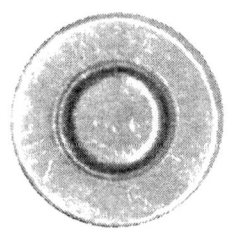

SPECIMEN DIMENSIONS

Rim Measurement: .528
Neck Measurement: .336
Bullet Diameter: .310
Case Length: 2.204

OTHER DETAILS

Caliber: .303
Manufacture Date: 1941
Specialty: Ball
Cartridge Type: Rifle / MG

Standard type round used during World War II

General Information: The bullet has a lead antimony core steel tipped with a cupro-nickel jacket. The powder is cordite and the primer annulus is varnished purple. Its muzzle velocity reached 2240 f.p.s.

UNITED KINGDOM

Arsenal: I.C.I. Kynoch (Imperial Chemical Industries)
Witton

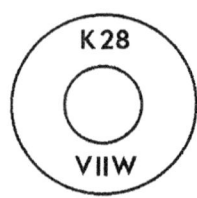

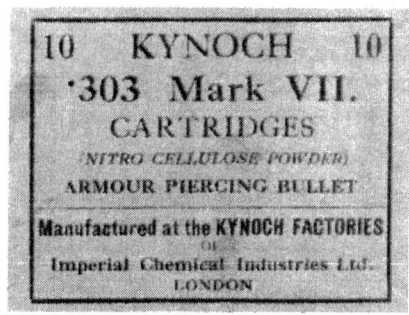

Headstamp   Side View

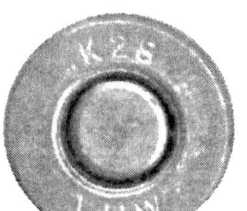

SPECIMEN DIMENSIONS

Rim Measurement: .526
Neck Measurement: .336
Bullet Diameter: .308
Case Length: 2.210

OTHER DETAILS

Caliber: .303
Manufacture Date: 1928
Specialty: Armor Piercing
Cartridge Type: Rifle / Mg

Standard type round used during World War II

General Information: The bullet is comprised of a hard steel core surrounded with a lead antimony alloy followed by a soft steel jacket coated with cupro-nickel. The powder used in this cartridge is nitro-cellulose and the primer annulus is green.

UNITED KINGDOM

Arsenal: I.C.I. Kynoch (Imperial Chemical Industries)
          Witton

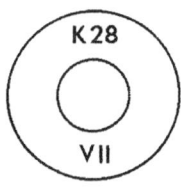

Headstamp

Side View

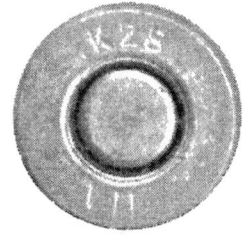

SPECIMEN DIMENSIONS

Rim Measurement: .528
Neck Measurement: .336
Bullet Diameter: .311
Case Length: 2.209

OTHER DETAILS

Caliber: .303
Manufacture Date: 1928
Specialty: Ball Air Service
Cartridge Type: Rifle / MG

Standard type round used during World War II

General Information: The projectile is comprised of lead antimony alloy with cupro-nickel jacket. The powder used in this "Air Service" cartridge is nitro-cellulose instead of the commonly used cordite. The round is easily identifiable by the purple primer annulus.

UNITED KINGDOM

Arsenal: I.C.I. Kynoch (Imperial Chemical Industries)
Witton

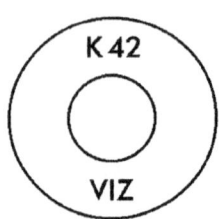

Headstamp

Side View

SPECIMEN DIMENSIONS

Rim Measurement: .525
Neck Measurement: N/A
Bullet Diameter: .402
Case Length: .745

OTHER DETAILS

Caliber: .455
Manufacture Date: 1942
Specialty: Ball
Cartridge type: Revolver

.455 Webley Revolver

General Information: This round was produced for the Webley officers model 1892/1905/1911 of Wilkinson, officially designated Mk VI. The Z indicates the cartridge is loaded with a non-corrosive powder. The bullet is comprised of lead antimony alloy with a cupro-nickel jacket. The primer annulus is purple.

UNITED KINGDOM

Arsenal: Royal Laboratory
          Woolrich, England

Headstamp

Side View

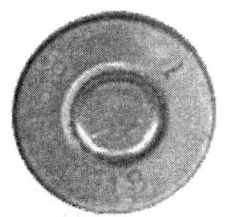

SPECIMEN DIMENSIONS

Rim Measurement: .530
Neck Measurement: .336
Bullet Diameter: .390
Case Length: 2.435

OTHER DETAILS

Caliber: .303
Manufacture Date: 1918
Specialty: Ball
Cartridge Type: Mg

.303 Lewis Machine Gun

General information: This round was developed for use in the Lewis machine gun and is easily identified by the steppe angle of the projectile. The T on the rim denotes the British headstamp letter code for black powder.

UNITED KINGDOM

Arsenal: Ministry of Supply Factory
Swynerton or Blackpool

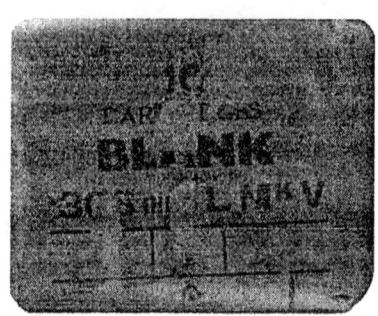

Headstamp   Side View

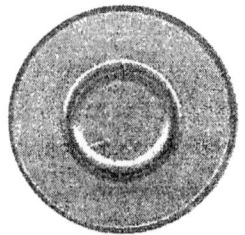

SPECIMEN DIMENSIONS

Rim Measurement: 531
Neck Measurement: 335
Bullet Diameter: N/A
Case Length: 1.844

OTHER DETAILS

Caliber: .303
Manufacture Date: 1944
Specialty: Blank
Cartridge Type: Rifle

General Information: This rifle grenade blank has an overall length of 2.295 with 6 petal crimps and no head stamp. Without the original packing the maker would most likely remain unknown.

NETHERLANDS

Arsenal: **Unknown**

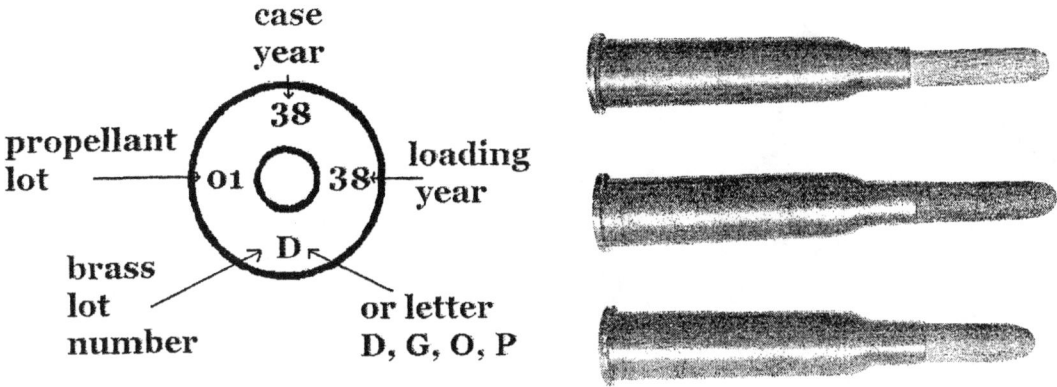

Headstamp

Side View

SPECIMEN DIMENSIONS

Rim Measurement: .526
Neck Measurement: .293
Bullet diameter: .247
Case Length: 2.114

Green Wood Blank

OTHER DETAILS

Caliber: 6.5
Manufacture Date: 1938
Specialty: Blank
Cartridge type: Rifle

Overall Length: 2.852

General Information   Most headstamps from this region contain all numerical elements that remain largely unidentified. Other headstamp examples with its corresponding manufacturers are listed on page 16 of this guide. Pictured above are two other versions of this blank, a plain wood bullet and a red stained one, but does the color have any significance as to type or function?

CZECHOSLOVAKIA
(German Occupation)

Arsenal: Waffenwerke Brun, Povazska, Bystrica,

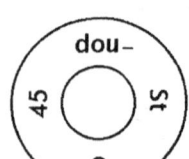

Headstamp

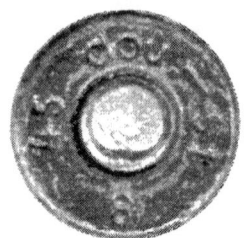

Side View

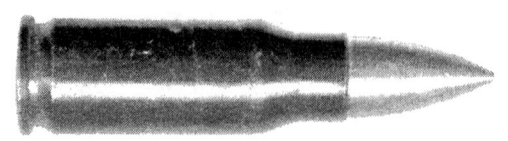

SPECIMEN DIMENSIONS

Rim Measurement: .466
Neck Measurement: .352
Bullet Diameter: .319
Case Length: 1.30

Kurz Patrone

OTHER DETAILS

Caliber: 7.9 x 33
Manufacture Date: 1945
Specialty: Practice Ball
Cartridge Type: SMG

Overall Length: 1.88

General Information: This cartridge largely developed by Polte and implemented during a late war period production for the Sturmgewehr-44, the worlds first assault rifle. The following manufacturers of Kurz ammunition have been noted during the late war period.

ak	Munitionsfabriken, Praha (Prague) (Czechoslovakia)
aux	Polte Armaturen und Machinenfabrik, Madgeburg, Sachsen
dou	Waffenwerke Brunn, Povazska & Bystrica (Czechoslovakia)
fva	Draht- und Metallwarenfabrik, Salzwedel
hla	Metallwarenfabrik Treuenbrietzen, Sebaldushof
kam	Hasag Eisen und Metallwerke, Skarzysko - Kamienna (Poland)
oxo	Teuto Metallwerke, Osnabruck
wa	Hugo Schneider, Lampenfabriken, Leipzig, Sachsen

CANADA

Arsenal: (DI) Defense Industries, Montreal, Quebec

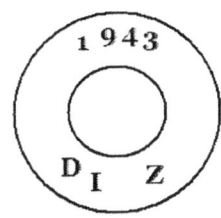

Headstamp

Side View

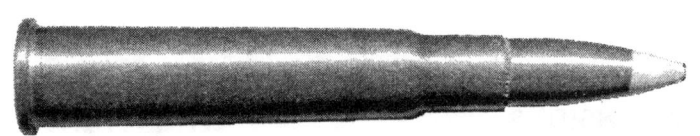

SPECIMEN DIMENSIONS

Rim Measurement: .523
Neck Measurement: .335
Bullet diameter: .308
Case Length: 2.212

.303 Tracer G4Z

OTHER DETAILS

Caliber: .303
Manufacture Date: 1943
Specialty: Tracer
Cartridge type: Rifle / MG

Overall Length: 3.35

General Information: This Canadian made tracer cartridge can be easily identified by its white tip and red primer annulus. The Z on the headstamp signifies that the powder in this round is non-corrosive. A table of color codes and designations for British & Canadian cartridges can be found on page 25 of this guide.

BELGIUM

Arsenal: Fabrique Nationale de Armes de Guerre, Herstal, Liege

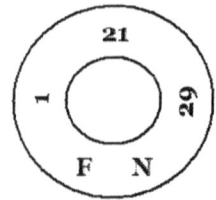

Headstamp

Side View

SPECIMEN DIMENSIONS

Rim Measurement: .528
Neck Measurement: .295
Bullet diameter: ..260
Case Length: 2.110

Tinned case & bullet

OTHER DETAILS

Caliber: 6.5x54Rmm
Manufacture Date: 1929
Specialty: Ball
Cartridge type: Rifle

Overall Length: 3.56

General Information: The specimen pictured above is one of many FN headstamp examples of this type cartridge. Listed below is a 1930s era variant headstamp that uses a letter code system to identify cartridge function as requested by a client.

B = Ball

SS = Hvy.Ball

T = Tracer

I = Incendiary

S = Lt.Ball

P = A P

PT = A P Tracer

E = Explosive

HEADSTAMP ALPABETICAL INDEX

	A	Altdorf
	A	American Cartridge Company, Kansas City, Missouri
	A A Co	American Ammunition Company, Oak Park, Illinois & Muscatine, Iowa
	A B & C Co.	American Buckle & Cartridge Company, West Haven, Connecticut
	A C	Armeria F.A. SC,San Cristobal
	A C & Co.	Austin Cartridge Company, Cleveland, Ohio
	A D	Angkatan Darat, (PSM) Turen, Maland, East Java
	A E	Arsenal do Ejercito, Lisbon
	A E = (E A)	Eretz Ayalon, Rehovot (Private "underground factory" Pre-Independence 1948)
	A E P	Anciens Etablissements Pieper, Herstal
	A F A	(Turkiye Cumhuriyeti) Askeri Fabrikalar Mamulati
	A H	Csepel Arsenal, Budapest
	A I	Artillerie Inrichtingen, Zandam
	A M	Armament et Munitiuni, Brasow
	A N	Twin Cities Ordnance Plant, Minneapolis, Minnasota
	A O	Allegany Ordnance Plant, Cumberland, Maryland
	A P X	Atelier de Construction de Puteaux, Puteaux
	A R S / R S	Atelier de Construction de Rennes, Rennes
	A T S / T S	Atelier de Construction de Tarbes, Tarbes
	A. A. Co.	Atlantic Ammunition Company, New York, N.Y.
	A.J.	Alton Jones, Portland, Oregan
	A.VIS	Atelier de Fabrication de Valance, Valence
	aak	Waffenfabrik Brunn, Prague, (Czechoslovakia)
	aan	Mitteldeutsche Metallwarenfabrik, Glauchau, Saxony
P-244	ab	Mundlos Nahmaschinenfabrik, Madgeburg-Neustadt
P-480	ac	Carl Walther Waffenfabrik, Zella-Mehlis, Thuringia
P-69	ad	Patronen-Zundhutchen und Metallwarenfabrik, Shoenbeck
	aek	F. Dusek Waffenzeugung, Opoczno Bei Nashod, (Poland)
	afu	August Winkhaus, Muenster
	ai	Unknown
	aj	Soerensen und Koester, Neumuenster
	ajf	Junker und Ruh, Karlsrue, Baden
	ajn	Union Sprengstoff und Zundmittel Werke, Alt-Beron
P-90D	ak	Munitionsfabriken, Praha (Prague) (Czechoslovakia)
	akv	Berg und Huettenwerksgesellschaft, Radotin, Prague
	al	Deutsche Leucht-und Signalmittelwerke, Dr. Feistel, Berlin-Charlottenburg
P-635	am	Gustloff-Werke Otto Eberhardt Patronenfabrik, Hirtenberg,

	anz	Machinen und Armaturenfabrik, Madgeburg
	ap	Deutsche Leucht-und Signalmittelwerke, Dr. Feistel, Wuppertal, Ronsdorf, Rheinland
	aqt	Otto Grusen und Company, Magdeburg
P-243	ar	Mauser-Werke, Berlin-Borsigwalde
P131	asb	Deutsche Waffen und Munitionsfabriken, Berlin-Borsigwalde
P-58	asf	Graetz Lampen und Metallwarenfabrik, Berlin
P-382	asr	Hanseatische Kettenwerk (HAK), Hamburg, Schleswig-Holstein
P-155	asw	E.F. Horster, Stahl-u. Metallwarenfabrik, Solingen
P-456	aue	Metall und Eisen, Nurnberg
P-270	auf	Metal Guss u. Presswerke H. Deihl, Nurnberg
	auj	Monheimer Ketten und Metallwaren-Industrie Poetz und Sand, Monheim-Dusseldorf
	auu	Patronenhulsen und Metallwarenfabrik, Rokycany, Pilsen (Czechoslovakia)
P	aux	Polte Armaturen und Machinenfabrik, Madgeburg, Sachsen
P-154	auy	Polte Armaturen und Machinenfabrik, Gruneburg, Nordbahn, (Poland)
	auz	Polte Armaturen und Machinenfabrik, Arnstadt, Thuringia
	av	Vereinigte Deutsche Metallwerke, Werdohl
	avk	Ruhrstahl, Brackwede-Bielefeld
P-414	avt	Silva Metallwerke, Madgeberg-Neustadt
P-345	avu	Silva Metallwerke, Genthin
P-222	awl	Union-Gesellschaft fuer Metallindustrie, Sils Van de Loo & Co. Werl-Frondenberg, Ruhr
P-152	awt	Wurtembergische Metallwarenfabrik, Geislingen, Steige, Wurttemberg
	axq	Erfurter Laden Industrie, Erfurt
	axs	Berndorfer Metallwarenfabrik, Amstettin (Austria)
	ay	Alois Pirkl Elektrotechn Fabrik, Reichenberg, Sudetenland
P-27	ayf	Erma, B.Geipel, Waffenfabrik, Erfurt, Thuringia
	azg	Siemens-Schuckert Werke, Berlin
	B	Bridgeport Brass Co., Bridgeport, Connecticut
	B	Pirotechnia di Bologna, Bologna
	B & M	Brass & Metall Manufacturing Co. Kansas City, Missouri (10.35mm Vetterli only)
	B / B C	Birmingham Metal and Munitions Co Ltd., Birmingham, Waltham Abbey, Essex
	B D	Halls Telephone Company, Burgfield
	B E	Royal Ordnance Factory, Swynerton, Blackpole, Worcester
	B F / 434	Bakelittfabrikken, Aurskog
	B K	Barutana Kamnik, Kamnik
	B M	British Munitions Company, London
	B N	Parc d'Artillerie de Place de Besancon, Besancon
	B N	St. Louis Ordnance Plant, St. Louis, Missouri
	B P D	Brombrini Parodi Defino, Rome - (AOC) contract for Egypt
	ba	Sundwiger Messingwerke, Iserlohn, Westfalen
	bb	A. Laue & Company, Berlin

	bc	Kupfer und Messingwerke, Langenberg, Rheinland
	bcd	Wilhelm Gusstloff Werke, Weimar, Thuringia
	bcd	Wilhelm Gustloff Werke, Weimar, Thuringia
	bd	Metallwerke Fa. Lange, Bodenbach, Sudetenland (Czechoslovakia)
	be	Berndorfer Warenfabrik, Berndorf, Niederdonau, (Austria)
	bf	Deutsche Rohrenwerke, Mulheim, Rheinland
	bg	Boehler & Company, Zweigniederlassung Edelstahlwerke, Berlin
	bh	Waffenfabrik Brunn, Povaszka, Bystrica, (Czechoslovakia)
	bj	Niebecker und Schumacher, Iserlohn, Westfalen
	bk	Metall- Walz und Plattierwarenfabrik, Wupertal
	bkp	Roehrenwerk Johannes Surman, Arnesberg
	bky	Bohmische Waffenfabrik, von Prague, Werk ung-Brod, Moravia, (Czechoslovakia)
	BLANCH	J. Blanch & Sons, London
	blp	Grazer Maschinen und Waggonbaufabrik, Graz
	blu	Sprengstoffwerke Blamau, Felixdorf
	bmv	Rheinmetall-Borsig, Sommerda, Thuringia
	bnd	Maschinenfabrik, Augsburg, Nuremberg
P-207	bne	Metallwerke Odertal, Odertal
P-186	bnf	Metalwerke Wolfenbuttel, Wulfenbuttel
P-452	bnr	Fr. Drabert Sohne Machinenfabrik, Minden, Westfalen
P-660	bnz	Steyr Daimler Puch, Steyr, (Austria)
P-963	bpr	Johannes Grossfuss Metal & Locierwarenfabriik, Dobeln, Sachsen
	bqt	Pirotechnische Fabrik Eugen Miller, Vienna, (Austria)
	BRMRC	British Manufacturing & Research Company, Grantham, Lincoln
	bt	Radiowerke Horny, Wien
	bvv	Rothmueller-Mewa, Wien
P-400	bwa	Gebruder Gabler Fingerhutz und Metallwarenfabrik, Schorndorf, Wurtemberg
	bwo	Rheinmetall-Borsig, Dusseldorf, Westfalen
	bwp	Berlin Anhaltische Maschinenbau, Dessau
	bxb	Skoda Werke, Pilsen, (Czechoslovakia)
	bxe	Bochumer Verein fur Guss-stalhlfabrikation, Bochum
	bxm	Vereinigte Zuender und Kabelwerke, Meissen
	byc	Aug. Klonne, Bruckenbauanstalt, Dortmund
	bye	Hannoversche Maschinenbau, Hanover
P-42	byf	Mauser Werke, Oberndorf am Neckar, Wurttemberg
	bys	Ruhrstahl,Guss-stahlwerke, Witten
P-75	byw	Johannes Schafer, Stettiner Schraubenwerke, Stettin, Pomerania
	bzt	Fritz Wolf Gewehrfabrik, Zella-Mehlis, Thuringia
	C B / C R B	Cartoucherie Belge, Liege Cartoucherie Russo Belge, Liege
	C - P	Crompton Parkinson Ltd., Doncaster, Yorkshire
	C / C.C.C.	Creedmore Cartridge Company, Barberton, Ohio
	C / P E C	Pirotechnia di Capua, Capua
	C A C	Colonial Ammunition Co., Auckland
	C B C	Companhia Brasiliera de Cartuchos, Sao Paulo
	C D L	C.D. Leet, Springfield, Massachusetts

	C F	Cartoucherie Francaise, Paris
	C I M	Consorcio de Industrias Militares 1932 -1936
	C M C / 21	Uzinale Metalwrgica di Corsa Mica SI, Cugir
	C N	Atelier Mechananique de Normandie, Normandy
	C N	Lake City Ordnance Plant, Independence, Missouri
	C O A	(Monogram) Industrias Quimicus "Duperial", Buenos Aires
	C P	Crompton Parkinson Ltd., Guiseley, Yorkshire
	C.C. Co.	Clinton Cartridge Company, Chicago, Illinois
	C.T.M. Co.	Crittenden & Tribbals Mfg. Company, South Coventry, Connecticut
P-287	can	A. Wallmeyer Machinenfabrik, Eisenach, Thuringia
	cbl	Vereinigte Deutsche Metallwerke, Nuremberg West
P-398	cdo	Theodore Bergmann & Co., Waffen und Munitionsfabriken, Velten am main
	cdp	Theodore Bergmann & Co., Waffen und Munitionsfabriken, Bernau, Berlin
P-147	ce	J.P. Sauer und Sohn Gewehrfabrik, Suhl, Thuringia
	cf	Westfalische Anhaltische Sprengstoff, Oranienburg, Brandenburg
P-249	cg	Finower Industrie, Finow/Mark, Brandenburg
	cgt	Josef Stefshy, Stockerau, Niederdonau
	ch	Fabrique Nationale d' Armes de Guerre, Herstal, Liege, (Belgium)
P-239	clc	A. Richard Herder Stahlwaren und Werkezeugfabrik, Solingen
	cnd	National Krupp Registrierkassen, Berlin
P-64	cnx	Gustav Appel Machinenfabrik, Berlin
P-175	cof	Carl Eickhorn Waffenfabrik, Solingen, Westfalen
	COLT	Colt Incorporated, Hartford, Connecticut
	con	Franz Stock Madchinen und Werkzeugfabrik, Berlin
	cos	Merz Werke, Gerbruder Merz, Frankfurt am main, Hessen-Nassua
	cpj	Havelwerke, Brandenburg
	cpo	Rheinmetall-Borsig, Berlin, Marienfeld
	cpo	Rheinmetall-Borsig, Berlin
	cpp	Rheinmetall-Borsig, Guben Werke, Brandenburg
	cpq	Rheinmetall-Borsig, Breslau, Silesia
	cr	Zander und optiz, Berlin
P-176	crs	Paul Weyersberg und Co., Waffenfabrik, Solingen, Westfalen
P-238	csd	Durkoppwerke, Bielefeld
P-178	csr	Gebruder Heller, Thuringia
	cts	Markisches Werke, Forge, Halver
P-174	cvl	WKC Waffenfabrik, Solingen-Wald
	cwg	Westfalische Anhaltische Sprengstoff, Coswig
	cxm	Gustav Genshow & Co., Berlin
	cyq	Spreewerke, Metallwarenfabrik, Berlin-Spandau
	cyw	Saechische Guss-stahlwerke Doehlen, Sachsen
	czo	Heeres-Zeugamt, Geschosswerkstatt, Konnigsberg, East Prussia
P-224	czs	Brennabor Werke, Brandenburg
	D	E.I. Dupont de Nemours Company, Pompton, New Jersey
	D / D R S	Dansk Rekylriffel Syndikat, Copenhagen
	D /D C /Co	Dominion Cartridge Co., Montreal, Quebec - Canadian Industries

		Ltd -
	D /GECO	Gustav Genchow & Company, Berlin
	D A	Dominion Arsenal, (C) Canada (Q), Quebec, (L) = Lindsay, Ontario
	D A G	Dynamit - Actien - Gesellschaft, Nuremberg
	D E N	Denver Ordnance Plant, Denver, Colorado (Remington Arms Co.)
	D F	Dum Dum Arsenal, Dum Dum, (Bengal) (Now Calcutta)
		DI NI SI
	D I / V C	Defense Industries, Montreal, Quebec V C = Verdun, Quebec
	D M	Danuvia Munitionsfabrik, Budapest
	D M	Deutsche Metallpatronenfabrik, Karlsruhe
	D M	Des Moines Ordnance Plant, Des Moines, Iowa (U.S. Rubber Co.)
	D o	Hirtenberg Patronenfabrik, Dordrecht
	D W A	Deutsche Werke Actiengesellschaft, Spandau /Berlin
	D W M	Deutsche Waffen und Munitionsfabriken, Karlsruhe
	D.C.Co.	Delaware Cartidge Company, Wilmington, Delaware
	DAM	Directoria da Marinha
	dbg	Dynamit, Duneberg
	dfb	Whilhelm Gustloff Werke, Suhl, Thuringia
	dgl	Louis Siegel, Sonneberg, Thueringen
	dgl*	Remo Gewehrfabrik, Gebruder Rempt, Suhl, Thuringia
	dma	Heeres-Munitionsanstalt und Geschosswerkstatt, Zeithain
P-151	dnf	RWS Rheinisch-Westfalische Sprengstoff, Nuremberg & Stadeln
P-405	dnh	Dynamit, Durlach, Karlsruhe
P-316	dom	Westfalische Metallindustrie, Lippstadt
P-945	dot	Waffenwerke Brunn, Brunn, (Czechoslovakia)
P-14A	dou	Waffenwerke Brunn, Povazska & Bystrica (Czechoslovakia)
	dov	Waffenwerke Brunn, Wsetin, (Czechoslovakia)
	dox	Waffenfabrik Brunn, Podbrezova, (Czechoslovakia)
	drv	Hasag Eisen und metallwerke, Tschenstochau (Czechoslovakia)
	dsh	Waffenwerke Inc. F. Jancek, Gewehrwerke, Prague-Nulse, (Czechoslovakia)
	DURA	Dura division of Detroit Harvester Corp., Toledo, Ohio
	dut	Spinnfleugelfabrik, Neudorf
P-237	duv	Berlin-Lubecker Maschinenfabrik, Lubeck, Schleswig-Holstein
	dve	Adolf Knoch, Saalfeld
	dwm	Liefergemeinschaft Dornbirn, Ludwig Rigger, Dornbirn
	dye	Erst Alpenlandische Pyrotechnik, Ed Pitschamann und Co., Innsbruck, (Austria)
P757	dyu	Heinrich Huppman Maschinenfabrik, Kitzgen-Etwashausen
	dza	Bleiwerke, Hamberg & Wilhelmsburg
	E	Yokosuka Naval Arsenal, Yokosuka
	E / ELEY	Eley Brothers Limited, London
	E C	Evansville - Chrysler Ornance Plant, Evansville, Indiana
	E C S	Evansville - Chrysler - Sunbeam Electric Ornance Plant, Evansville, Indiana
	E I D	Etablissements Industriels de Defense, Damascus

	E K	Eastman Kodak, Rochester, New York
	E K/E N K	Greek Powder and Cartridge Co., Athens (German contract)
	E W	Eau Claire Ordnance Plant, Eau Claire, Wisconsin (U.S. Rubber Co.)
P-379	eba	Metallwarenfabriken Scharfenberg & Teubert, Breitungen-Werra, Thuringia
	ebk	Machinenbau und Bahnbedarf, Spandau, Babelsberg
	eca	Oscar Fischer, Baden
	ecc	Pyrotechnische Fabrik, Mohringen
	ecd	Earl Lippold Pyrotechnische Fabrik, Wuppertal-Elderfield, Rheinland
	edg	Henckels Zwillingswerke, Solingen
P-413	edq	Deutche Waffen- und Munitionsfabriken, Lubeck & Schultup
P-327	eds	Zuendappwerke, Nuernberg
	eeg	Herman Weihrauch, Gewhr und Fahrradteilfabriken, Zella-Mehlis, Thuringia
	eeh	F. Soennecker, Bonn
P-315	eej	Markisches Walzwerke, Stausberg, Bez- Potsdam
	eem	Selve Kronbiegel, Dornheim & Sommerda
	eeo	Deutche Waffen- und Munitionsfabriken, Posen, West Prussia
P-198	eey	Metallwarenfabrik Truenbrietzen, Roederhof
P-120	emp	Dynamit, Alfred Nobel, Empelde, Hanover
P-346	eom	H. Huck Metallwarenfabrik, Nurnberg, Bavaria
	eun	Rana-Werke, Klardorf, Oberpfalz
	evz	Bergbau, Salzgitter
	exp	Landes-Lieferungsgenossenscaft des Tischlerhandwerks, Bezirk, Westfalen
P-423	exq	Clemens Kreher Metall-Blechspielwaren-u. Trommelfabrik, Marienberg
	exw	Metallwerke Holleischen, Sudetenland
	eyd	Heidenreich und Harbeck, Hamburg
	F A B / 22	Fabrica di Armamant Brascow, Brascow
	F C I	Fabrica de Cartuchos Itajuba, Minas Gerais
	F C P Q	Fabrica de Cartuchos e Polvoras Quimicas, Chelas
	F DE M/FM	Fabrica Nacional de Municiones, Sante Fe
	F M S L	Fabrica Militar de Cartuchos de San Lorenzo, San Lorenzo
	F N	Fabrique Nationale de Armes de Guerre, Herstal, Liege
	F N C M	Fabrica Nacional de Cartuchos e Municoes, Sao Paulo
	F N M	Fabrica Nacional de Municoes de Armas Ligeiras, Moscavide
	F R / R	Fabrica Realengo, Rio de Janeiro
	F.GY. BP.	Fehyvergyar Budapest, Budapest
	F.W.L. Co.	F.W. Lamplough & Company, Montreal, Quebec
	F/F A/FAL	Frankford Arsenal, Philadelphia, Pennsylvania (SL* tools removed from St.Louis)
	F/FC	Federal Cartridge Company, Anoka, Minnesota
	fa	Mansfeld, Hettstedt, Sud/Harz, Sachsen-Anhalt
P-28	faa	Deutche Wafen- und Munitionsfabriken, Karlsruhe
	FAMAP	Fabrica Argentina de Municiones de Armas Portatiles, San Larenzo
	FAMMAP	Fabrica Argentina de Militar de Municiones de Armas Portatiles, San

		Larenzo
	FAMMAPB	Fabrica Argentina de Militar de Municiones de Armas Portatiles, Borghi
	FAPS	Frankford Arsenal Pirotechnic Signal, Philadelphia, Pennsylvania
P-334	fb	Mansfield, Rothenberg/Saale
	fde	Dynamit, Foerde
	feh	Machinenfabrik Donauwoerth, Donauwoerth
P-491	fer	Metallwerke Wandhofen, Schwerte
	feu	Krone Presswerke, Berlin
P-240	ffc	Friedrich Herder Stahlwarenfabrik, Solingen
	FFV	Forenede Fabriksverken Vanasverken, Karlstad, Varmland
P-416	flp	Heintze & Blankertz, Erste Dutsche Stalhlfederfabrik, Werk Oranienburg, Berlin
	FMCSF	Fabrica Militar de Cartuchos de San Francisco
	fnh	Bohmische Waffenfabrik, Prague, Strakonitz, (Czechoslovakia)
	fnk	Adolf Hopf, Tambach-Dietharz, Thuringia
	FNT / P	Fabrica National de Toledo, Toledo P=Palencia
P-359	foy	Horn Tachometerfabrik, Leipzig
P-457	fpo	H. Meinecke, Breslau
P-208	fsa	Federstahl, Kassel
P-132	fva	Draht- und Metallwarenfabrik, Salzwedel
	FVV & Co.	Fitch Van Vechten & Company, New York, NY
	fwh	Norddeursche Machinenfabrik, Hauptverwaltung, Berlin
P-122	fxo	C.G. Haenel Waffen und Fahrradfabrik, Suhl, Thuringia
	FYA	=contract (P=Polte) (HP=Hirtenberg)
	fze	F.W. Holler Waffenfabrik, Solingen, Westfalen
	fzs	Heinrich Krieghoff Waffenfabrik, Suhl, Thuringia
	G /G B	Greenwood & Batley, Leeds
	G 18 F 1	Government Factory, #1, Blackheath
	G A	Grenfell & Accles, Birmingham
	G C D	G. C. Dornheim, Suhl
	G E	General Electric Co., Cleveland, Ohio
	G F 3	Government Factory, #3, Blackpole
	G F L	Giulio Fiocchi, Lecco
	G S F	Societe Francaise des Munitions, Issy - les - Moulineaux
	ga	Hirsch Kupfer- und Messingwerke, Finow/Mark
	gal	Wagner und Company, Muehlhausen, Thuringia
	GBF	Greenwood & Batley, Farnham
	GEVELOT	Gevelot & Gaupillat Freres, Paris
	ghf	Fritz Kiess und Company Waffenfabrik, Suhl
	gpt	Gustav Bittner, Weipert, Sudetengau
	gqm	Loch und Hartenberger, Idar-Oberstein
	GR	G. Roth, Wien und Pressburg
	gsb	Rheinmetall-Borsig (Des Ateliers De La Dyle), Louvain, (Belgium)
	gsc	S. A. Belge de Mecanique et de le Armament, Mecar, (Belgium)
	gtb	J.F. Eisfeld und Pyrotechnische Fabriken, Guntersberg
	guy	Werkzeugmaschinenfabrik Oerlikon, Buhrle und Company, Zurich,

		(Switzerland)	
	H	Hokuto Shinto Kabushiki Co.	
	H	Halls Telephone Company, Dowlais	
	H	Hirtenberger Zundhutchen u. Patronenfabrik, Hirtenberg (Austria)	
	H A / A A	Haerens Ammunitionsarsenalet (Army Ammunition Arsenal), Copenhagen 1938-1950	
	H L	Haerens Krudtvaerk (Army Laboratorium), Copenhagen 1900-1937	
	H N	Royal Ordnance Factory, Hirwan, South Wales	
	H.B.Fisher	H.B. Fisher, Philadelphia, Pennsylvania	
	ham	Dynamit, Hamm	
P-169	has	Pulverfabrik Hasloch, Hasloch-am-main	
	hew	Waffenfabrik Inc. F. Jancek, Pangrac, (Czeckoslovakia)	
	hgs	W. C. Gustav Burmeister Pyrotechnische Fabrik und Signalmittelwerke, Hamburg	
	hhg	Rheinmetall-Borsig, Berlin-Tegel	
P-340	hhw	Metallwerke Silberhutte, St. Andreasberg/Harz	
	hhx	M. Boehme, Grosshartmannsdorf, Sachsen	
	hhy	Louis Ulbricht, Rosenthal, Erzgebirge	
P-25	hla	Metallwarenfabrik Treuenbrietzen, Sebaldushof	
P-163	hlb	Metallwarenfabrik Treuenbrietzen, Selterhof	
P-442	hlc	Zieh- und Stazwerke, Schleusingen	
P-198	hld	Metallwerke Treuenbrietzen, Belsig/Mark, Brandenburg	
	hle	Metallwerke Treuenbrietzen, Roederhof	
	hrk	Schluermann und Company, Westfalen	
P-162	hrn	Presswerk, Metgethen, East Prussia	
	hta	Koenig und Company, Wein	
P-185	i	Elite Diamantwerke, Chemnitz	
	I C I	Imperial Chemical Industries Limited, Birmingham	
	I F S	International Flare & Signal Co., Tippercanoe City, Ohio	
	I K	Igman Konjic, Konjic	
	I M	Industria Militar, Bagota	
	I M I / T Z	Israeli Military Industries, Tel Aviv Taasiya Tsviat	TZ / TZZ -
	I M P A	Industria Metallurgica y Plastica Argentina	
	I V I	Industries Valcartier, Inc., Quebec	
	J- CH	Chuo Kayaku Kako Kaisha Co.	
	J- S T	Showa-Kayaku, Inc., Tsuruoka	
P-265	ja	R. und G. Schmole Metallwerke, Menden, Westfalen	
	J-AO (A)	Asahi Okuma Arms Corporation, Asahi	
	jhv	Metallwaren, Waffen und Maschinenfabrik, Budapest, (Hungary)	
	jkg	Koenig Staatliche Eisen Stahl-und Maschinenfabrik, Budapest, Hungary	
	jry	Hermann Herthold, Olbernhau, Sudetenland, (Czechoslovakia)	
	J-T E / T E	Toyo Seiki Manufacturing, Company, Ltd., Tokyo	
	jtb	S. A. Tavaro, Ghent, Belgium	
	jua	Danuvia Waffen und Munitionsfabriken, Budapest, (Hungary)	
	jwa	Manufacture de armes Chatellerfault, Chatellerfault, (France)	

K	Kynoch, England 1916 contract
K	Karlskrona "Karlsborg" Naval Arsenal, Karlskrona, Blekinge
K 2	Kynoch, Imperial Chemical Industries Limited, Standish
K 4	Kynoch, Imperial Chemical Industries Limited, Yeading, Hayes, Middlesex
K 5	Kynoch, Imperial Chemical Industries Limited, Kidderminster, Worcestershire
K A	Government Arsenal, Pusan
K B W	Kathodion Bronze Works, Nyack, NY
K F	Kirkee Arsenal, Kirkee, (Bombay) (Now Maharahtra)
K H	Khamaria Arsenal, Jubbulpore, (Central Provinces) (Now Madhya Pradesh)
K N	Kings Norton Metal Company Limited, Abby Wood, Kent, London
K S	Allegheny Ordnance Plant, Cumberland, Maryland (Kelly Springfield Tire Co.)
K V	Krusik Valjevo, Valjevo
K/KYNOCH	Kynoch, Imperial Chemical Industries Limited, Birmingham
kam	Hasag Eisen und Metallwerke, Skarzysko - Kamienna (Poland)
keb	Jiranek und Company, Brunn
kfa	Statliches (Sarajevo State Arsenal), Sarajevo (Yugoslovia)
kfg	Gesellschaft zur Verwertung chemischer Erzeugnisse, Kaufering
kfk	Dansk Rekylriffel Syndicat, Kopenhagen, (Denmark)
klb	J.F. Eisfeld Pulver und Pyrotechnische Fabriken, Kieselbach, Thuringia
kls	Styer Daimler Puch, Warsaw (Poland)
krl	Dynamit, Afred Nobel und Company, Kruemmel, Koblenz
kry	F. A. Sening, Hamburg
ksb	Manufacture National d' Armes de Lavallois, Paris (France)
kum	Hartmann und Braun, Frankfurt am-main
kun	J.F. Eisfeld Pulver und Pyrotechnische Fabriken, Kunigunde
kur	Steyr Daimler Puch, Furhofstrasse, Graz, (Austria)
kwm	S. A. Fiat, Turin, (Italy)
kye	Fabrica de Armamant Brascow, Brascow, (Roumania)
kyn	Armament et Munitiuni, Brasow, (Roumania)
L	Lorenz Ammunition and Ordnance Company, Millwall, London
L	Ludlow and Company, Wolverhampton, Staffs
L B C	Leon Beaux & Company, Milan
L C	Lake City Ordnance Plant, Independence, Missouri (Remington Arms Co.)
L D F	Liberty Display Fireworks Co., Danville, Illinois
L M	Cartoucherie du Mans, Le Mans
L M / R L	Lowell Ordnance Plant, Lowell, Massachusetts (U.S. Ctg. Co.)
L V E / 188	Novosibirsk Low Voltage Equipment Plant, Novosibirsk
ldb	Deutsche Pyrotechnische Fabriken, Malchow, Mecklenburg
ldc	Deutsche Pyrotechnische Fabriken, Cleebron, Wurtemburg
ldn	Deutsche Pyrotechnische Fabriken, Neumarkt, Schlesien
LIBERTY	Liberty Cartridge Company, Mt. Carmel & Sioux City, Connecticut

lkm	Sellier & Bellot Munitionsfabriken, Praha (Praque) (Czechoslovakia)
lwg	Optische Werke, Osterode, Harz, Westfalen
M	Munizioni e Cartucce Martignoni, Genoa
M	Mariestad "Marieberg, Kungsholmen" Arsenal, Mariestad, Skaraborg
M	Milwaukee Ordnance Plant, Milwaukee, Wisconsin
M / T	Standard Electrica, Madrid
M A X I M	Maxim Munitions Corporation, Waterton, New York
M F	Small Arms Ammunition (Government) Factory No. 1, Footscray
M F / 21	Matravideki Femmuvek, Sirok
M F S	Munitions Factory, Sundari
M G	Small Arms Ammunition (Government) Factory No. 2, Footscray
M G	Marcel Gaupillat & Company, Paris
M H	Small Arms Ammunition (Government) Factory No. 3, Hendon
M I	Societe Meridionale d' Industrie, Marseille
M J	Small Arms Ammunition (Government) Factory No. 4, Hendon
M K E	Makina ve Kimya Edustrisi, Kuruma
M L / 23	Magyar Loszermuvek RT, Veszprem
M M	Besa 7.92x57 machinegun also 9mm - sten gun 1942-45
M M D	Government Arsenal Contract (EID), Damascus
M M M	Manufacturas Metalicus Madrilenas (case)
M Q	Small Arms Ammunition (Government) Factory No. 5, Rocklea
M R	Manufacture de Machines du Haut-Rhin, Mulhouse-Bourtzwiller
M S	Small Arms Ammunition (Government) Factory No 7, Salisbury
M W	Small Arms Ammunition (Government) Factory No. 6, Welchpool
M W	Munitionswerke, Shoenbeck-am-elbe
M W S	Munitionswerke, Shoenbeck-am-elbe
M Z K	Miloje Zadic, Krusevac
M.F.A. Co.	Meridan Firearms Mfg. Company, Meriden, Connecticut
MAXIM	Maxim Arms Company, London
MESKO /21	Solidnosc Knokurencyjnosc Otwartosc, Zaklady Metalowe, Skarzysko-Kamienna
MM	Ministry of Marine
moc	Johann Springers Erbrn Gewehrfabrikanten, Vienna, (Austria)
mpr	Hispano Suiza, Geneva (Switzerland)
mrb	Aktiengesellschaft Skoda Werke, Prague-Smichow, (Czechoslovakia)
myx	Rheinmetall-Borsig, Sommerda, Thuringia
N	Rheinische- Westfalische- Sprengstoff, Nuremberg
N	Panstwowe Wytwornie Uzbrojenia, Fabryka Amunicji, Skarzysko-Kamienna
N A Co	Newton Arms Company, Buffalo, New York
N B / 24	Norrhammars Bruk
N C	National Conduit & Cable Co. Hastings on the Hudson, New York/became NCI
N C I	National Brass & Copper Tube Co. (National Conduit) Hastings on the Hudson, N.Y.
N W M	Nederlandsche Wapen en Munitiefabriek, 's Hertogenbosch, North Brabant

na	Westfalische Kupfer- und Messingwerke, Ludenscheid
nbe	Hasag Eisen und Metallwerke, Apparatbau Tschenstochau
ndn	Heinrich Bluecher, Fabrik technic Buersten, Spremberg
nea	Walther Steiner Eisenkonstructionen, Suhl, Thuringia
nec	Waffenwerke Brunn, Werk Gurein, Prague, (Czechoslovakia)
nfx	RWS Munitionsfabrik, Warsaw, (Poland) & Praha, (Praque) (Czechoslovakia)
nhr	Rheinmetall-Borsig, Sommerda, Thuringia
NOEN	Naval Ordnance Engineering Laboratory, Dalhlgren, Maryland 20mm Oerlikon
None	Imperial Japanese Army Arsenal, Tokyo
Norma /27	Norma Projektilfabrik, Amotfors, Varmland & Oslo, (Norway)
nrh	Johannsen und Zieger, Oranienburg
NS / NRC	China North Industries, Beijing
nyv	Rheinmetall-Borsig, Unterluess, Hanover
O F N	Ordnance Factory Nigeria, Lagos
O F V	Varangaon Arsenal, Bhusawal
O R B E A	Cartucheria Orbea Argentina
oxo	Teuto Metallwerke, Osnabruck
oyj	Alteliers de Construction de Tarbes, Tarbes (France)
P	Aichi Naval Arsenal, Aichi
P & S	Potz & Sand, Mulheim
P C	Kings Mills Ordnance Plant, Kings Mills, Ohio (Peters Cartridge Co.)
P C Co	Peters Cartridge Company, Ohio
P C H	Poudres (Powder) Carttoucherie (Cartridge) Hellenique (Greek) Co., Athens
P G	Probjeda Gorazde, Gorazde
P K	Pocisk, Spolka Akcyjna, Warsaw
P M P	Pretoria Metal Pressings, Pretoria
P P U / 11	(PP) Prvi Partisan, Titovo, Uzice
P S	Povaske Strojarne, Povaska, Bystrica
P S M	Pabrik Senjasta Mesiu, Turen, Maland, East Java
P S/PMC	Poongsan Metal Manufacturing Company (Angang Facility), Seoul
P.	Polte, Madgeburg
PETERS	Peters Cartridge Company, Cincinnati, Ohio
pjj	Haerens Ammunitionsarsenalet, Copenhagen, (Denmark)
pla	Unknown
pmu	Unknown
PMV/13	Government Arsenal, Havana
Q C	Qui-Nhon Cartridge Co., Qui Nhon
qa	William Prym, Stollberg, Rheinland
qlv	Unknown
qnw	Unknown
qrb	Sezione del Pirotechico, Bologna (Italy)
qve	Carl Walther Waffenfabrik, Zella-Mehlis, Thuringia
r	Westfalische Anhaltisch Sprengstoff, Reinsdorf
R A	Remmington Arms Company, Bridgeport, Connecticut

R A H	Remmington Arms Company, Hoboken, New Jersey	
R A S	Remmington Arms Company, Swanton, Vermont	Formerly RHA Co (1917)
R A / A Y R	Raufoss Ammunisjonsfabrikker, Raufoss	
R C / R H	Raleigh Cycle Co., Ltd., Nottingham	
R D	Armeria F.A. SC, San Cristobal	
R F	Rockland Fireworks Co., Boston, Massachusetts	
R G	Ministry of Supply Factory, Radway Green	
R L	Royal Laboratory, Woolwich, Kent, London	
R M S	Rheinische Metallwaren und Maschinenfabrik, Sommerda	
R R Co	Ross Rifle Company, Montreal, Quebec	
R T A	Royal Thai Army Arsenal, Bangkok	
R T S	Richard Threlfall & Sons (explosive anti-zeppelin cartridges only)	
R W	Rudge Whitworth Limited, Tyseley	
R W S	Rheinische Westfalische Sprengstoff, Nuremberg	
R Y	Establissements Rey Freres, Nimes	
R/R H A Co	Robin Hood Ammunition Company, Swanton, Vermont	
ra	Deutsches Messingwerke C. Eveking, Berlin	
rde	Unknown	
REM-UMC	Remmington Arms - Union Metallic Cartridge Co., Bridgeport, Connecticut	
rhs	Rheinmetall-Borsig, Soemmerda	
rtl	Pulverfabrik, Koln-Rottweil	
S	Koenigliche Munitionsfabrik, Spandau	
S	Solothurn	
s	Dynamit, Alfred Nobel, Werke Lumbrays	
S L	St. Louis Ordnance Plant, St.Loius, Missouri	
S & W	Smith & Wesson Ammunition Company, Rock Creek, Ohio	
S /P S	Pirotecnia Militar de Sevilla, Seville, Sevilla	
S /S O	Suojeluskuntain se-je Konepa ja Oy (SAKO), Riihimaki	
S A	Government Arsenal, Cartagena 1936 - 1939	
S A	Savage Arms Corporation, Chicopee Falls, Massachusetts	
S A Corp	Savage Arms Corporation, Chicopee Falls, Massachusetts	
S A W	Sage Ammunition Company, Middletown, Connecticut	
S B	Sellior & Bellot, Schoenbeck	
S B	Sociedad Santa Barbara, Oviedo	
S B / P	Sellier & Bellot, Prague (Praha)	
S B.T	Sociedad Santa Barbara, Toldedo	
S C	Sloboda Cacak, Cacak	
S C C	Standard Cartridge Company, Pasadena, California	
S D	Sparklet Devices Inc., Dover, Ohio	
S d/PMC	Poongsan Metal Manufacturing Company (Dongrae Facility), Seoul	
S E	Staatliche, Erfurt	
S F M / S F	Societe Francaise des Munitions, Issy - les - Moulineaux, Paris	
S K D	Selve - Kronbiegel - Dornheim, Suhl	
S M / 26	Swenska Metallverken, Stockholm (Amf = Armeforvaltningen - Army procurement)	

	S M Co	Stant Manufacturing Co., Connersville, Indiana
SYI / CT	S M I	Societa Metallurgica Italiana, Campo Tizzore
	S P	Scorzato, Lujan
	S P C	Sociadade Portuguesa de Cartucheria
	S R	Royal Ordnance Factory, Aycliffe, Spennymoor
	S T	Royal Ordnance Factory, Steeton
	S. E	Munitionsfabrik Stettin, Stettin, Prussia
	S.C.Co.	Southern Cartridge Company, Savannah, Georgia
	skd	Selve Kronbriegel, Dornheim, Suhl
	So.C.Co.	Southern Cartridge Company, Houston, Texas S.C.Co. = Savannah, Georgia
	Speer	Vernon D. Speer, Lewiston, Idaho
	suk	Deusche Waffen u. Munitionsfabriken, Karlsruhe-Durlach
P-42	svw	Mauser Werke, Oberndorf am Neckar, Wurttemburg (supplemental components P-s42)
P-959	swp	Mauserwerke (Waffenwerke Brunn), Brunn, Brno, (Czechoslovakia)
P-160	t	Dynamit, Alfred Nobel, Troisdorf, Rheinland
	T	Toyokawa Naval Arsenal, Tokyo
	T	Thun
	T	Tulskia (Tula) Patron (Cartridge) Zavody (Works), Tula
	T	Pirotechnia di Torino, Torino
	T A	Tel Aviv Arsenal (Israeli Military Industries), Tel Aviv (9mm export only)
	T A	Thai Arms, Bangkok
	T C F S	(Turkiye Cumhuriyeti) Fabrikalar Iskenderun, Iskenderun (Alexandretta)
	T C/T W	Twin Cities Ordnance Plant, Minneapolis, Minnesota (Federal Cartridge Co.)
	T E	Cartoucherie de Toulouse, Toulouse
	T E I	Triumph Explosives Inc., Elkton, Maryland
	T H	Trefeleries et Laminoirs du Havre, Le Havre
	T M	Sezione del Pirotechico, Bologna
	T R	Three Rivers (Dominion Rubber Munitions Ltd.), Three Rivers, Quebec
	ta	Duerener Metallwerke, Berlin
	tjk	Unknown
	tpk	Unknown
	tpn	Unknown
	tvw	Unknown
	U / U	South African Mint (SAM), Pretoria & Kimberly
	U F	United Fireworks Co Manufacturing Co., Dayton, Ohio
	U M C	Union Metallic Cartridge Company, Bridgeport, Connecticut
	U S	United States Cartridge Company, Lowell, Massachusetts
	U/U T	Utah Ordnance Plant, Salt Lake City, Utah (Remington Arms Co.)
	ua	Osnabrucker Kupfer- und Drahtwerke, Osnabruck
P-67	unt	H. Unttendorfer, Munitionsfabrik, Nuremberg, Bayern

BAO	V A F / 10	Durjava (VoennA Fabrika), Kazanlak
	V C	Defense Industries, Verdun, Quebec
	V E	Cartoucherie de Valance, Valence
	V F M	Vitale Fireworks Manufacturing Co., New Castle Pennsylvania
	V M T	Valtion Metallitehtaat, Helsinki (VALMET)
	V P T / P T	Valtion Patruunatehdas, Lapua
	V S	Parc d'Artillerie de Place de Verdun, Verdun
P-94	va	Kabel- und Metallwerke Neumeyer, Nuremberg
	VFM & CA	Capsulerie Leigoise, Francotte, May & Cie, Liege
	W R A Co.	(WRA) (Winchester) Winchester Repeating Arms, New Haven, Connecticut
	W/W C C	Western Cartridge Company, East Alton, Illinois
P-181	wa	Hugo Schneider, Lampenfabrik, Leipzig, Sachsen
P-128	wal	Wolf & Co. Walsrode, Hannover
P-370	wb	Hugo Schneider, Berlin & Kopenick
P-797	wc	Hugo Schneider, Meuselwitz, Thuringia
	wd	Hugo Schneider, Taucha, Sachsen
	we	Hugo Schneider, Langeweissen, Thuringia
	WESTERN	Western Cartridge Company, East Alton, Illinois
	wf	Hugo Schneider, Hasag Eisen u. Metallwerke, Kielce (Poland)
P-490	wg	Hugo Schneider, Altenberg, Thuringia
	wh	Hugo Schneider, Eisenach, Thuringia
	WISE	Wise Manufacturing Company, Watertown, New York
	wj	Hugo Schneider, Oberweissbach, Thuringia
	wk	Hugo Schneider, Schlieben, Sachsen-Anhalt
	wn	Hugo Schneider, Dernbach, Thuringia
	xa	Busch-Jager, Ludenschneider Metallwerke, Ludenscheid
	y	Jagdpatronen, Zundhutchen u. Metallwarenfabrik, Budapest (Hungary)
	ya	Sachsische Metallwarenfabrik, Aue in Sachsen
	Z	Buhrle & Company, Zurich (Oerlikon)
	Z / ZV(3B)	Cesklovenska Zbrojovka Akciova Spolecnost v Brne, Brno, Bystrica
	zb	Kupferwerk Ilsenberg, Ilsenberg, Harz

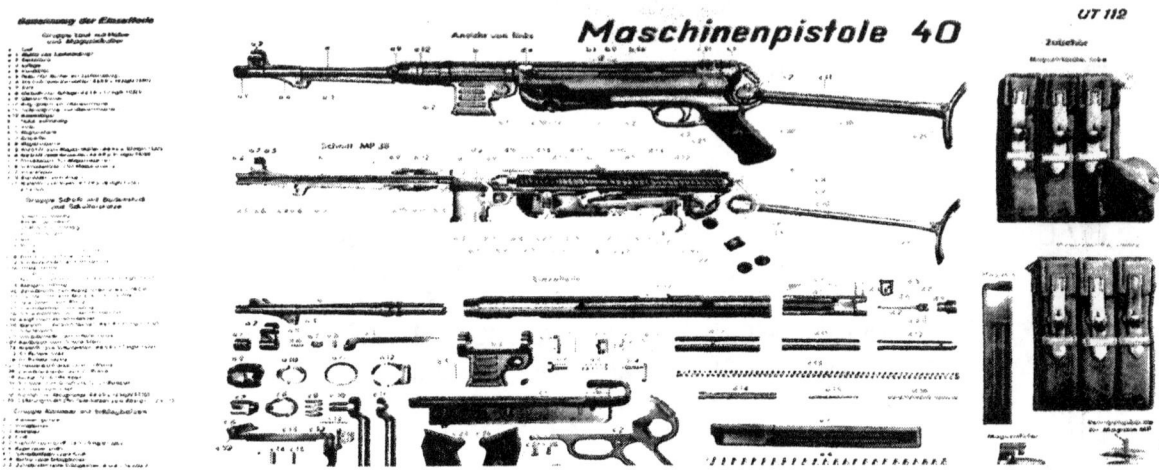

GERMAN PATRONEFABRIKEN CODE

P	Polte Armaturen und Machinenfabrik, Madgeburg, Sachsen
P-14A	Waffenwerke Brunn, Povazska & Bystrica (Czechoslovakia)
P-25	Metallwarenfabrik Treuenbrietzen, Sebaldushof
P-27	Erma, B.Geipel, Waffenfabrik, Erfurt, Thuringia
P-28	Deutche Wafen- und Munitionsfabriken, Karlsruhe
P-42	Mauser Werke, Oberndorf am Neckar, Wurttemberg
P-42	Mauser Werke, Oberndorf am Neckar, Wurttemburg (supplemental components P-s42)
P-58	Graetz Lampen und Metallwarenfabrik, Berlin
P-64	Gustav Appel Machinenfabrik, Berlin
P-67	H. Unttendorfer, Munitionsfabrik, Nuremberg, Bayern
P-69	Patronen-Zundhutchen und Metallwarenfabrik, Shoenbeck
P-75	Johannes Schafer, Stettiner Schraubenwerke, Stettin, Pomerania
P-90D	Munitionsfabriken, Praha (Prague) (Czechoslovakia)
P-94	Kabel- und Metallwerke Neumeyer, Nuremberg
P-120	Dynamit, Alfred Nobel, Empelde, Hanover
P-122	C.G. Haenel Waffen und Fahrradfabrik, Suhl, Thuringia
P-128	Wolf & Co. Walsrode, Hannover
P-131	Deutsche Waffen und Munitionsfabriken, Berlin-Borsigwalde
P-132	Draht- und Metallwarenfabrik, Salzwedel
P-147	J.P. Sauer und Sohn Gewehrfabrik, Suhl, Thuringia
P-151	RWS Rheinisch-Westfalische Sprengstoff, Nuremberg & Stadeln
P-152	Wurtembergische Metallwarenfabrik, Geislingen, Steige, Wurttemberg
P-154	Polte Armaturen und Machinenfabrik, Gruneburg, Nordbahn, (Poland)
P-155	E.F. Horster, Stahl-u. Metallwarenfabrik, Solingen
P-160	Dynamit, Alfred Nobel, Troisdorf, Rheinland
P-162	Presswerk, Metgethen, East Prussia
P-163	Metallwarenfabrik Treuenbrietzen, Selterhof
P-168	Pulverfabrik, Koln-Rottweil
P-169	Pulverfabrik Hasloch, Hasloch-am-main
P-174	WKC Waffenfabrik, Solingen-Wald
P-175	Carl Eickhorn Waffenfabrik, Solingen, Westfalen
P-176	Paul Weyersberg und Co., Waffenfabrik, Solingen, Westfalen
P-178	Gebruder Heller, Thuringia
P-181	Hugo Schneider, Lampenfabrik, Leipzig, Sachsen
P-185	Elite Diamantwerke, Chemnitz
P-186	Metalwerke Wolfenbuttel, Wulfenbuttel
P-198	Metallwarenfabrik Truenbrietzen, Roederhof
P-198	Metallwerke Treuenbrietzen, Belsig/Mark, Brandenburg
P-207	Metallwerke Odertal, Odertal
P-208	Federstahl, Kassel
P-222	Union-Gesellschaft fuer Metallindustrie, Sils Van de Loo & Co. Werl-Frondenberg, Ruhr
P-224	Brennabor Werke, Brandenburg

P-237	Berlin-Lubecker Maschinenfabrik, Lubeck, Schleswig-Holstein
P-238	Durkoppwerke, Bielefeld
P-239	A. Richard Herder Stahlwaren und Werkezeugfabrik, Solingen
P-240	Friedrich Herder Stahlwarenfabrik, Solingen
P-243	Mauser-Werke, Berlin-Borsigwalde
P-244	Mundlos Nahmaschinenfabrik, Madgeburg-Neustadt
P-249	Finower Industrie, Finow/Mark, Brandenburg
P-265	R. und G. Schmole Metallwerke, Menden, Westfalen
P-270	Metal Guss u. Presswerke H. Deihl, Nurnberg
P-287	A. Wallmeyer Machinenfabrik, Eisenach, Thuringia
P-315	Markisches Walzwerke, Stausberg, Bez- Potsdam
P-316	Westfalische Metallindustrie, Lippstadt
P-327	Zuendappwerke, Nuernberg
P-334	Mansfield, Rothenberg/Saale
P-340	Metallwerke Silberhutte, St. Andreasberg/Harz
P-345	Silva Metallwerke, Genthin
P-346	H. Huck Metallwarenfabrik, Nurnberg, Bavaria
P-359	Horn Tachometerfabrik, Leipzig
P-370	Hugo Schneider, Berlin & Kopenick
P-379	Metallwarenfabriken Scharfenberg & Teubert, Breitungen-Werra, Thuringia
P-382	Hanseatische Kettenwerk (HAK), Hamburg, Schleswig-Holstein
P-398	Theodore Bergmann & Co., Waffen und Munitionsfabriken, Velten am main
P-400	Gebruder Gabler Fingerhutz und Metallwarenfabrik, Schorndorf, Wurtemberg
P-405	Dynamit, Durlach, Karlsruhe
P-413	Deutche Waffen- und Munitionsfabriken, Lubeck & Schultup
P-414	Silva Metallwerke, Madgeberg-Neustadt
P-416	Heintze & Blankertz, Erste Dutsche Stalhlfederfabrik, Werk Oranienburg, Berlin
P-423	Clemens Kreher Metall-Blechspielwaren-u. Trommelfabrik, Marienberg
P-442	Zieh- und Stazwerke, Schleusingen
P-452	Fr. Drabert Sohne Machinenfabrik, Minden, Westfalen
P-456	Metall und Eisen, Nurnberg
P-457	H. Meinecke, Breslau
P-480	Carl Walther Waffenfabrik, Zella-Mehlis, Thuringia
P-490	Hugo Schneider, Altenberg, Thuringia
P-491	Metallwerke Wandhofen, Schwerte
P-635	Gustloff-Werke Otto Eberhardt Patronenfabrik, Hirtenberg, Niederdonau, (Austria)
P-660	Steyr Daimler Puch, Steyr, (Austria)
P757	Heinrich Huppman Maschinenfabrik, Kitzgen-Etwashausen
P-797	Hugo Schneider, Meuselwitz, Thuringia
P-945	Waffenwerke Brunn, Brunn, (Czechoslovakia)
P-959	Mauserwerke (Waffenwerke Brunn), Brunn, Brno, (Czechoslovakia)
P-963	Johannes Grossfuss Metal & Locierwarenfabriik, Dobeln, Sachsen

BIBLIOGRAPHY

Technical Manual TM 43-0001-27 U.S. Army Ammunition data sheets, June 1981

Small Caliber Ammunition, FSC 1305

G. Roth Ammunition catalog June 1890

Handbook of Enemy Ammunition," London, 1943-44

Handbook of Italian Military Forces," Washington, 1943

Japanese Explosive Ordnance," Washington, 1943

RWS Ammunition-Sinoxide," Nuremberg, 1939

DWM – Katalog." Karlsruhe, 1904

Textbook of ammunition," London, 1936

Defense Intelligence Agency "Small Caliber Ammunition Identification Guide"
DST 1160G 514 81 Vol. 1 Amended / By Albert Watson, III
August 1984

Ordnance Department, U.S. Army, Small Arms Ammunition
"A History of an Industry", 1918 – 1944 Vols I & II, 1944

The information contained in this guide reflects my personal notes as a collector of cartridges for the past 10 years and is derived from the first hand examination of cartridges and both U.S. and Foreign technical manuals. Some entries have also been added due to the generous contributions of stories and information by my fellow collectors over the years.

See guys, I was paying attention…sometimes

www.ingramcontent.com/pod-product-compliance
Lightning Source LLC
Chambersburg PA
CBHW060315240426
43661CB00059B/2773